TELL YOUR STORY

Build your brand
and grow your business

HOLLY CARDAMONE

Cover design, internal design and copy editing: Lauren Shay – Full Stop Writing, Editing and Design.

For Gabriella and Alessia –
there's nothing I love more than watching your story unfold.

Contents

CONTENTS

Acknowledgements

I've poured over twenty years of communications and professional writing experience and expertise into the pages of this book. I couldn't have written it without my incredible network of clients, colleagues, friends and supporters that I've cultivated over the past two decades and beyond. I am blessed with extraordinary people who lift me in more ways than I could ever possibly count, and not just because my maths skills are beyond horrific.

A special mention of gratitude must go to the jaw-droppingly phenomenal Thriving Women, headed up by our fearless and formidable yet endlessly kind and generous leader, Emma McQueen. Emma's grace, vision and steadfast belief in unlimited possibilities is uplifting, challenging and ultimately soul-affirming. Emma and the Thriving Women compel me to think big, reign it in when need be, and be open to growth in ways I had never before contemplated. Their collective insights, intelligence and sheer intellectual gold have transformed my work, my business and my life. What can't I do without that tribe of superstars in my corner?

My Mum and Dad and my brother Saher were my first storytellers, are my biggest fans yet harshest critics (in all the good ways!) and the appreciation I have from an idyllic childhood on a farm on the beach, steeped in bloody good literature, can never be adequately expressed.

It's a truth universally acknowledged that I have the best husband in the history of husbands. Endlessly encouraging and supportive, he's somewhat patiently waited over 15 years for me to publish a book and become the next JK Rowling – sorry, lover, this is a book, but it's not *the* book. Keep waiting!

Finally, to my beautiful daughters, Gabriella and Alessia. You're two somewhat feisty, endlessly curious, funny, strong, clever and kind girls. You have gifts the world needs. Dream big, dream hard and tell your stories.

INTRODUCTION

My Story

Make yourself something heavily caffeinated (or juice up some leafy greens if you're so inclined), slip into something comfortable (stretchy yoga pants for the win) and settle in for my story from employee to employer of self.

Once upon a time, there was a girl who wore killer heels and a suit every day, who had a fulltime job in the CBD working as a communications advisor, managing multi-million dollar projects, while completing a Master of Arts (Communications), and then a Master of Arts (Professional Writing and Literature) – that girl was me. I had a non-fiction lecturer who liked the way I strung words together, and encouraged me to pitch articles for publication, and wouldn't you know it, they were accepted! By day, I wrote speeches, letters, policy papers, articles, communications strategies and corporate communications collateral, and by night, I wrote poetry, personal narratives and feature articles about many topics, including men's underwear.

Around the same time, the project I was working on finished, and after many years of working in a bureaucracy, I desperately needed a change. I booked a holiday to Italy for the following year and set myself the challenge of earning enough money through freelance writing and communications to be able to do nothing but eat gelato and lie on a southern Italian beach for a month.

But let's start at the beginning. I've always loved writing and reading. My dream growing up was always – *always* – to be a writer. Along came Year 12, and my beloved English Literature teacher pulled me aside and advised me to change my uni preferences from a stock-standard (but oh, so desirable) Arts degree to an Applied Science Nursing degree. She told me that writers need life experience, and that nothing would give better exposure to life experience than working with people at their most vulnerable. I changed my preferences, was accepted into Monash University's nursing program, and dragged myself through four years of something I had absolutely no passion for with a long-term plan to go back to university ASAP, collecting both cash and stories along the way.

Given the nature of health care in general, and the public health sector in particular, there was certainly no shortage of stories falling into my lap. I was the nurse that would sit on people's beds, braid their hair, massage their hands and chat. My first professional writing job was in a nursing home, now, rightfully so, referred to as an 'aged care facility'. My part-time job through university was at a hideous facility in Melbourne that was eventually closed down – thank goodness – and turned into apartments. I worked there from 5–9pm, Monday to Friday, for three years, and my main job was to walk around the facility after the evening meal collecting twenty-seven sets of dentures, often straight from people's mouths, and almost always with a fair bit of creative persuasion. I'd scrub them and then put them back on their bedside table ready for the morning. Yep, highly glamorous stuff. For months, night after night, I watched the nurse in charge struggle to squeeze out half a page of notes to describe a month's worth of care for a person. One evening, having finished the heady task of wrestling with my body weight in dentures, I asked her if I could do it with or for her. I wrote four pages in around twenty minutes, and from then on, monthly care reporting and planning became my responsibility. My monthly care reports were mini novels. Imagine, if you dare, the most overly descriptive care notes you've ever seen in your life. I'm talking bowel movements portrayals that Charles Dickens would be proud of, descriptions of wounds that a surgeon could treat remotely just on description alone, and notes that would make any non-nurse, AKA a normal person, vomit into their handbag. Oh yes, like any writer who knows how to elicit a response and convey a scene with accuracy and more than a little flair, much, much more than was necessary, I used all five senses. Writing was my favourite part of the three years I spent working there.

The next step along my writing journey was obtaining a Communications Master's. I completed it while doing communications temp work interlaced with night duty in aged care facilities across Melbourne, before being offered a government position to manage a multi-million-dollar communications campaign. I generally don't believe in luck: I believe in hard work and consistency. However, I firmly believe Lady Luck was smiling down upon me at that time. You see, the department I was working for held a working lunch with a group of recruiters and temp agencies, one of which was sending me on short-term communications and writing gigs. At the lunch, the host described a tricky position to fill. They needed a communications and writing specialist who had high-level insight and insider knowledge of nurses and nursing. Tick, tick, tick! Overnight, I went from writing up nursing care plans with far too many verbs and adjectives, to working on the most successful government campaign of all time, while writing a Master's thesis about the perilousness of online health information.

That was a long, long time ago. Now I have my own business and work with a fabulous mix of clients from corporate, not-for-profits (NFPs) and philanthropic organisations, as well as small, mostly service-based businesses. I absolutely love working with small businesses: I love their drive, their commitment to what they do, and I'm completely, utterly besotted with helping people tell their story and grow their business with beautiful communications.

I've been working as a communications specialist and a professional writer for over 25 years now (sheesh!). In fact, my business, Blue51 Communications, started life as Holly Cardamone Communications and Freelance Writing. In this capacity, I wrote freelance pieces for magazines, journals and newspapers while balancing contract and project roles with large organisations, mostly government agencies. Before that, and in between launching Blue51 Communications, I worked as communications manager and as director for a number of different organisations. I also brought a couple of cherubs into the world as well (no mean feat).

It's those two said cherubs that largely influenced my why and my brand story.

I wasn't sure I'd like being my own boss – I'm someone who loves a checklist and a process, but I discovered working for myself allowed me to nurture my need to organise, plan and make lists. It also allows me to set my own goals, untied to a broader, relatively faceless organisation. I can work on my passions and my motivations, rather than the targets set by the 22nd floor. I love working on a diverse mix of projects, and working on the projects that appeal to me. A communications and writing consultancy provides the opportunity to work with inspirational clients on exciting projects, solving their communications problems to achieve tangible, in some cases life-changing results in their businesses. What's not to love?

Blue51 Communications

Blue51 Communications is a boutique communications consultancy with one core focus – the power of story. I wholeheartedly, emphatically believe that words are at the heart of good communications. The whole crux of my business, inclusive of all of my services (communications advising, strategy and writing for business) is helping my clients communicate better with their audience. Bottom line: I help people in business say something (i.e. their story) and have that message heard by their intended recipient.

When I rebranded as Blue51 Communications, a huge part of my 'why' was walking the tightrope between my work and my family commitments. Here's the thing – the working mama juggle ain't always a big bucket of champagne. Work/ life balance makes an appearance on a lot of company profiles – I should know, I write them. In reality, I know that it can be an illusion. I'm not suggesting that there's no such workplace as one that has true flexibility; I'm sure there are plenty. I also know from my experience and those of my working mama friends that truly flexible workplaces are a rare and much-coveted breed. If my cherub is up for a student of the week award and I want to go witness that moment of seeing her eyes light up, then damn it, I'm not running that by anyone. However, that's not the main why I started this business; the *why* why, if you will.

I wasn't particularly familiar with the world of small business (other than other freelancers such as graphic designers and web developers) until my last in-house communications role. I managed communications for an NFP membership organisation, where a lot of their client base were people with small businesses. When word got out that I was leaving, a number of members contacted me for outsourced communications and writing support for their own small businesses. These were people who had seen how I had transformed that organisation's communications and wanted to see what magic I could work on theirs.

I caught a glimpse of a need requiring fulfilment ... it was less of a glimpse and more of a big, fat gaping hole in the market. A fabulous opportunity for my work life had just materialised completely unbidden. It really struck me that there was a need for no BS communications and writing services that cut to the core of what a business needs, and excluded all the crap that they didn't (highway overpass advertising, I'm looking at you).

But, who to offer my skills and expertise to? The diversity of a client mix appealed to me greatly opposed to the relative static environment of in-house communications. People who were approaching me had fantastic business offerings but lacked effective messaging to get their ideal client to take notice of them and see their value. There are a lot of people who lack the skillset in communications to showcase their business effectively.

Rather than work with just anyone, I wanted to be considerate and deliberate about who I worked with. A couple of key clients cemented this – I decided I only wanted (and am still committed to this) to work with people who are doing good stuff out in the world in their special zone of bliss. It's very Jerry McGuire-esque, but more than anything, I wanted to be inspired in my work life.

Boom! My why, what and who clarified! Now, what to call this mofo and close off this brand story?

At least once a month, I'm asked about the story behind my business name, Blue51 Communications. I was on holiday on a beautiful tropical South Pacific island, reflective and serene, when the word 'blue' kept rising to the forefront. Blue water, blue skies, blue cocktails. Blue is calming and ordered yet makes an indisputable impact. Think of a splash of blue against a white backdrop, or the slash of a white cloud on a blue sky. Packs a punch, yes?

Without getting too esoteric or woo-woo (soooo not me!), blue is the colour of water, the sea and the sky with all the associated symbolic references of calm, peace, stability, security and loyalty. It's associated with depth and stability, symbolising trust, wisdom, confidence, intelligence, faith, truth and integrity. While in my communications I make sure clichés are avoided like the plague (get it, get it, see what I did there?), they often have a basis in an elemental truth. Blue skies are emblematic of optimism, creativity and opportunity and are full of positive meaning in almost every culture – after all, we live on the blue planet. It was decided. The word 'blue' had to be front and centre of my refreshed business name.

As for the meaning of 51, I wish I could give you a symbolic reference to the deeper intention of numerology, but alas. They're a pair of numbers that at the time were the respective favourites of two cherubs I know.

Blue51 Communications is my business name. My tagline is 'tell your story'. Why? Because nothing connects like a good story, and as a Word Nerd, story is at the heart of all my communications.

Why this book?

Like a true Type A, I really enjoy working with clients to make sure their communications and marketing plans closely align to their strategic business plans, that the messages they send out effectively reach the people they most wish to connect with. At the same time, we smash their business goals right in the throat – bam!

People in business often have massive creativity, impeccable services and unique ideas, but when it comes time to convey their attributes in writing, they get tangled up in jargon or stilted, 'professional' best Year 11 essay language. It's true – a lot of business writing is bad. Excruciatingly so. This book is for people who:

- Feel too close to their work for the objectivity to share their message accurately and effectively in writing.

- Know that their written words aren't working as hard as they should.

- Love what they do but need help to polish their message.

- Know their long-held attachment to jargon and industry lingo is impenetrable and confusing to their mother, let alone potential clients.

- Find it really difficult to explain on paper both what they do, and the benefits they could genuinely bring to peoples' lives.

Through this book, I share some of the key strategies I use in my work every day, both in terms of communications writing and weaving stories through communications tactics. As you read, my goal is for you to scribble like mad. Deface the following pages in any way that you find useful as you create your plan of attack to showcase your brand – personal and business – in the best possible light through smart, engaging communications and storytelling. I want you to approach your business communications like a writer, and I'll give you the tools to translate your messages and points of difference into a story that reflects you and your work accurately, effectively and purposefully.

Bottom line? This book will give you a plan, (wo)man. A plan for you to go forth, and write like you are the Communications Director of your brand, because, let's face it, you are. There's no-one better placed than you to be telling your story.

Let's jump in, shall we?

PART ONE

Tell Me a Story

Holly Cardamone

CHAPTER ONE

The Power of Communications

At the core, communications are how you expose yourself to the world. Done well, your brand and business values are clearly articulated, your client feels aligned to your ethos and you are smug in the knowledge that the messages you put out into the world reflect you accurately.

I'm astounded by organisations and businesses that don't regularly communicate with their clients or audience, especially when it's quite simple to do so. Social media strategies are easy to implement, websites are ubiquitous, and I can't think of many businesses that I interact with regularly that don't have a blog, newsfeed feature or newsletter built into their communications schedule.

As a business, you need to get the word out, fast. You need to get your brand out there: you have a message but you don't have a megaphone, nor a spare $800 million. Communications to the rescue! I'm talking strategic, deliberate, ongoing, targeted, considered messaging hitting the right audience in the most effective way.

Communications are where all the fun stuff lies – it's where we celebrate! Communications can also be an effective way to solve a problem. They provide an opportunity to get creative, to work around limited budgets and to get some serious mileage in terms of brand exposure and smash overarching goals. More than anything else, though, communications are essential to a successful, sustainable business. Actually, scrap that: good communications are the difference between disseminating information about your business and having people connect with your message in a way that builds an ongoing relationship with you.

Here's the thing: people are completely and utterly swamped with information. Your business – your services, benefits and value – could be the very answer to their prayers, but without a strategic approach to getting your message across, there is little chance of them receiving and understanding your communications.

A communications plan with story as a central focus significantly increases the chance of your message landing at the right place at the right time. It confirms and clarifies your key messages, the people you want to reach and work with, and the best way to deliver those messages.

What is business writing?

Have a think about all the writing that crosses your desk each and every workday. There are pieces of content that are, well, if not a delight to read, are at least readable. They prompt you towards action. Then there's content that is right up there with a colonoscopy.

Common issues are:

- Weak structure
- An introduction that doesn't make sense or is too abstract
- Repetition that's just annoying
- Sentences that are far too long or, alternatively, too short and blunt
- Passive writing
- Content that is jargonistic, dense and difficult to read
- Gaps in the information
- No clear call to action

What makes good business writing? A message that's:

- Tied to a broader business goal
- Logical and clear
- Compelling and on brand
- Evocative of the brand voice

Planning

Planning sometimes makes creative, spontaneous types break out in a cold sweat, but honestly, without a plan, the potential for a rambling mess of a project is increased tenfold. The first step in planning out a project is having a vision, a strong idea of what the finished piece will look like. Before you even begin writing, you need to ask some key questions:

- What do I want to say, and why?
- Why should my target audience care about this?
- Will it drive my business?

Holding a mirror to your communications

It's really, really difficult to look objectively at one's own business communications. How does your business look from the outside? Your business communications are broader than your services, products or offerings. They speak to your strengths, your experience and the benefits you offer. All your business communications – your copy, logo, website, emails and social media – tell a story about your business. Are your messages clear and compelling? Is the way you communicate your business aligned and reflective of your values? Are your communications aligned to those of your ideal client?

There are a number of ways to look at your communications from the outside, but an easy(ish) way is to take the perspective of your ideal client and how they engage with your touchpoints. This can be an incredibly valuable exercise.

I've had some people tell me they rely solely on word of mouth marketing for their business. I'm a massive fan of providing service so exemplary that your clients do your marketing for you. However, keep in mind, the vast majority of people, when given a recommendation by a trusted friend or family member, will head straight to Dr Google to check out your business. What happens when someone googles you and your business? You want to look as good, as professional as your clients are telling their friends you are.

Communications check up

- **Does your business email have a Gmail or Hotmail address rather than a dedicated URL?**
  Most hosting packages come with email hosting as part of the deal – mine certainly does, so if yours doesn't, have a shop around.

- **Does your website have an about page with a clear and engaging brand story?**
  It doesn't have to be *Pride and Prejudice*, but your about page should include copy that covers the who, why, how and what.

- **How's your imagery?**
  If you don't love your photos, or if you don't have any at all, consider investing in a branding shoot with an amazing photographer.

- **Do you use different colours, fonts, sizing and tones across your website, social media or email campaigns?**
  That's an easy fix, my pretty. If you're not particularly visual (I'm not), engage a designer to create a visual style for you, specifying the fonts and colours that best suit your branding, and apply them religiously across your business communications.

Effective communications relies on one main thing: clarity. Yes, clarity. Without a solid dose of clarity, business communications end up as one big, splattered, confusing mess of messages, audiences and purposes.

Clarity in purpose means you're never just putting out tactics for the sake of it. Your tactics (social media, blogging, events, networking) become tied to a greater purpose, and you can align them to three main subcategories: to be inspiring, educational and entertaining (where appropriate).

Clarity in messaging keeps writing and tactics targeted. When messages are simple and aligned to broader business clarity, relevance is almost guaranteed, and it becomes much easier to address audience pain points.

Clarity in audience means you can consistently deliver tactics and content that your client can connect with and relate to, and very quickly see you as the answer to their clearly articulated problems.

All three – purpose, messaging and audience – will guide your tactics, the means by which you connect an audience with a message. Is blogging right for you, for your audience? It won't be if reading blogs are not part of your audience's everyday life.

Creating a business vision

Have you ever been to an art class? I've dabbled in some workshops on and off over the years, but as someone who is completely non-visual, someone who completely, wholeheartedly, undoubtedly and ABSOLUTELY sucks at Pictionary, I find them, quite frankly, terrifying. Every class I've ever been to has always started with what can only be described as a pep talk delivered in a nurturing, relaxed tone. I have more than my fair share of visually creative arty-farty friends (as I affectionately call them), and when I've asked them how they start with a blank canvas and end up with a gorgeous piece, they all start with some variation of a story that has been doing the rounds of art classes since JC himself played full forward for Jerusalem, as my gorgeous dad would say:

> *An artist is about to sculpt an elephant from a huge chunk of stone.*
>
> *An interviewer asks her, 'How will you turn that rock into an elephant?'*
>
> *'Easy,' says the sculptor, 'I just take off the bits that don't look like an elephant.'*

So, too, with writing for your business.

Strategic plans. Spreadsheety-business types love them, with their KPIs, their SWOTs and their WTFs ... OK, so I added in that last one, which is perhaps best ignored and definitely not googled.

These documents are often the guiding principles by which businesses and organisations operate, and usually a lot of work goes into their development by a lot of different people. Particularly in the NFP sector, strategic plans are an essential component of business cycles and often attached to funding mechanisms. Strategic plans are quite different across industries, but at their core, they highlight:

1. Where a business is at a particular point in time
2. Where they want to be in the future (i.e. their vision)
3. The gaps between two and three above
4. The strategies they will implement to bridge the gaps

I don't know about you, but that's enough to bring a tear to my eye. Undertaking a strategic plan exercise is valuable for all businesses, not just big-uns. By their very nature, they force you to nail down a vision. Once the strategies are determined to achieve a vision, a communications plan comes into play: the roadmap to communicate the vision.

A fabulous communications plan aligns target audience, key messages and ideal channels with the overarching aim of meeting business vision and goals. It integrates strategy with tools, activities and evaluation methods and builds a brand, and grows a business. It gives a clear framework to get your message directly to your dream client. There's a whole lot of idea-bouncing and brainstorming, tweaking of existing business communications, and a ton of clarity, direction, a renewed sense of communications inspo.

My clients have distinct goals and strategies for their businesses, but often feel like they lack the communications skills to showcase what they do in a way that their ideal client responds to. It's so important to have a communications strategy that is aligned to the broader strategic business plan. A good strategy will have the information and detail for implementation over time, and result in a tangible air of smugness, knowing that a business is supported by strong, effective communications.

A dance across touchpoints

We have contact! There are multiple ways a person comes into contact with your brand and your business, and a business that successfully and compellingly tells their story also ensures their business has consistent, accurate and compelling communications across almost all touchpoints.

There are many ways to market your business, but rather than try everything to see what sticks, pick a number of essential tactics or strategies that are aligned to touchpoints, i.e. that make sense to the way somebody typically comes across your business, and do them well. I usually advise on five touchpoints to focus on, and the five will complement each other and are manageable in the day-to-day of running a business.

Your five touchpoints could be:

- Website and SEO
- Social media
- Mailing list
- Branding, particularly important for businesses with a physical location
- Event schedule, including external events such as networking and conferences

Now, here's the kicker: make sure that there's consistency in communications across all of your touchpoints. What does this mean exactly? The voice that's on your website should be the voice that you use in your social media captions, and when someone meets you at a networking event, there's no disconnect between your online persona and the real-life experience of speaking with you. The pitch you deliver verbally about your work and your services should echo the information that you've included in your website copy.

'So, Holly, oh, wise one,' I hear you cry. 'How do we get consistency?'

We plan for it!

CHAPTER TWO

Communications Planning

No-one likes an ill-thought-out scattergun approach, hoping something will stick – no, a communications roadmap is a much preferable way to manage business communications.

Fact – I love a detailed plan for my business communications that goes into the usual who, what, why, where and how of my business. However, if you're about to launch a new service or product or host an event, a one-page quicky communications roadmap will align your project to your overall communications, as well as calm overwhelm.

First step – get yourself a large piece of butcher paper, some bright pantone markers or Sharpies, and either a tie-dye voluminous dress, or a crisp, white cotton shirt, depending on your branding.

Second step – have someone take a carefully curated shot of you in your tie-dye/cotton shirt ensemble and post it to Instagram, using the hashtag #goaldigger.

Third step – laugh uproariously at the two steps above.

Grounding – not just for yogis

Just as blue is the new black, it seems for many of us working mamas juggling cherubs and business, February is the new January. And, of course, there can be no January, faux or otherwise, without a ton of business planning, now can there?

Every January, my Instagram feed is chock-a-block full of images of goal setting for the year ahead.

Here's the kicker, though – unless there's clarity around business goals, it's really hard to set robust communications goals.

Communications goals are intrinsically linked to your broader business goals and overarching vision. When communications goals are aligned with business goals, they become grounded, strategic and targeted by default, with a focus on the end result, which is usually tied to business performance measures, such as client growth and income targets. Any and every communications goal needs to have that bigger picture in mind, and move the business towards its vision.

Communications, at the core, is about getting your business message in front of those who need to hear it. The act of creating communications goals demands focus – what do you actually want to happen from each communications activity? Why?

Let's say your business goals for the next twelve months are to double your sales of your favourite service, or to fill out your 1:1 services, or to consistently sell out events to cement your positioning as a thought leader, or to increase your overall sales by 10% to make you the market leader in your industry.

Your communications goals are going to be focused on tactics that help you achieve these broader goals:

- Increased social media followers on a specific platform (communications goal) will build awareness to sell out an event or specific service-stream (business goal).

- An improved client experience (communications goal) will increase your client retention rate (business goal).

- A website update with an extensive FAQ page (communications goal) will reduce admin time (business goal).

- An article published in a women's health magazine (communications goal) will increase access and exposure to your target audience of fit women (business goal).

Communications goal setting

Communications goals are a way to confirm and clarify the response you want from your communications and how you want your brand and business reflected. There's an art and a science to writing goals, and everyone (and their grandmother) is familiar with the SMART process, but I'm gonna spell it out again, 'cause I wanna.

Write your goals in a way that is:

S – specific
M – measurable
A – attainable
R – relevant
T – time-based

I recently came across another acronym which is a bit more fun and passion-driven. Say hello to HARD goals:

H – heartfelt (tell me what you want, what you really, really want)
A – animated (can you clearly visualise what achieving this goal looks like?)
R – required (includes steps that must be achieved to keep momentum and progression)
D – difficult (complex enough to keep you sweating and engaged, rather than bored)

Regardless of whether your communications goals are SMART or HARD, bottom line – write them down and measure them!
The process can be convoluted, but I like to keep things simple when setting communications goals – I'm good like that.

• What is the business trying or wanting to achieve?
• What are the communications goals that will meet this?
• What are the strategies, tactics and actions which will do this?
• How will success be measured?

Would you like an example? Of course you would!

Business A is a health and fitness centre and wants to focus on filling their group training classes as a means to achieve a financial target (business goal). The communications goals to achieve this are brand and service awareness, increase in lead generation and conversion, and positioning Business A as a business that helps their clients achieve staggering transformations. The strategies, tactics and actions Business A will implement to achieve their communications goals are a social media strategy with a Facebook ad campaign, an email campaign targeting former clients, an email campaign with a promotion for existing clients to refer a friend, and attendance at a local community event. The measures of success that Business A will look for are an increase in social media followers, and increase in list sizes, and of course, the number of people sweating it up in their classes each day.

Setting communications goals with the end business goals in mind keeps your communications activities focused and targeted. The messages you put out via your tactics – social media, website copy, even your pitch – are addressing and meeting your overarching business goals.

Banging out a quick one-page communications plan

Here's a quick guide to bashing out a basic communications and marketing plan for the next twelve months, preferably on a large piece of butcher paper using bright pantone markers and some washi tape. Please note – there's no theoretical basis for the second part of that sentence other than it looks good on Instagram.

1. Define your what in one sentence – what you do/offer/sell.

2. Define your who – your dream client/customer that needs your what (i.e. your services and products as above).

3. Write a quick blurb or series of dot points outlining the best way to make Numbers one and two meet and do the tango:

   • Client touchpoints (social media, advertising, marketing tools, PR).

   • Calls to action including sharing messages, and directing clients to a dedicated page on your website.

   • Retention strategy (how you keep your ideal client engaged with you).

- Growth strategy for continuing to attract more of your ideal client.

4. Plot all of number three against a calendar, clearly specifying when you are going to undertake each element.

5. Go forth and communicate, my pretty.

Quiz time!

What's the most essential element when it comes to telling your story? Is it a touch of devilishly handsome antagonist, thrill seeking, or an epiphany *Eat Pray Love* style?

Wrong, wrong, wrong …!

It's a misconception that drama and intrigue are the core of any good story. Sorry to disappoint, but it's something much less exciting. You ready? Clarity! Whoop, there it is again! Clarity is possibly the most important quality of good business writing – or any writing, really. Clarity demands complete understanding of what it is you specifically want to say. Without clarity, there can only be confusion and misunderstandings, or people giving up on your message.

Related to clarity is the concept of purpose. This means answering that ol' chestnut: 'What's in it for me?' Do your services or products make your ideal client's life easier, less stressful, more enjoyable?

Having a clear understanding of your target audience or dream client is essential in order to create beautiful, effective business writing.

32 | *Holly Cardamone*

CHAPTER THREE

Fine-Tuning Your Brand Story

'Tell your story' is my business tagline. More than a tagline, it's the core of my brand story, the essence of what I do through my communications and writing for business. It guides everything I do in terms of the services I offer and my communications and marketing.

A good brand story will share how and why your business was established, your motivations, drivers, criteria for success – both yours and the people you serve. Basically, it provides an insight into your work and the people involved, both as providers and recipients, and the relationship between the two, in the context of the benefits your work provides others.

I love writing brand stories, and I think they're important to use in your communications toolkit. They enhance and facilitate connection and engagement, essential to building relationships. It's an articulation of your values, the core of your work, and so it's not a set and forget task to tick off. You'll use iterations of your brand story across all of your business communications, from your website (not just your about page!), your social media posts, your marketing and sales funnels, your client work process – in fact, your entire client experience journey should emulate your brand story.

Are your business values aligned with your brand story?

There was a specific brand that permeated my adolescence and early twenties that was cooler than cool. It's not a stretch to say that it played a big part in informing my career choice of communications, all while keeping my skin well moisturised without using products tested on animals. The brand was headed up by a formidable, pure dynamo of a woman that all the girls in my Year 12 cohort wanted to be when we grew up. They used marketing campaigns that compelled us to protect the planet, support community fair trade, defend human rights, support rights for women and remove blackheads. Can I get a hell yeah?

A decade or two passed, and imagine my dismay when walking past one of their stores with my cherubs to see an image bigger than my house of a naked man hiding his bits with a bar of (cruelty-free glycerine) soap. There can be no denying the model was sporting an admirable set of abs, but explicit exploitation, sexualised images and objectification were a considerable disconnect from the brand's former, long-term focus on unshakable ethics.

Sex sells; there's nothing new about that. But it doesn't have to, and for the vast majority of brands and businesses, it's inappropriate, unnecessary and unacceptable to buy into the increasing overexposure of sexual advertising.

Brand story

I'm all about the practical and action based, so here are some examples and tips for sharing your brand story:

- Write out your brand story (the who, the what, the why) in the first person wherever possible. As we'll explore later, first person point of view resonates and is engaging.

- Turn this into a blog post or copy for your about page – after giving it a decent edit, of course!

- Write a set of at least five key messages that fall out of your brand story and align these to the different services/arms of your business and what you do. These will become prompts for your social media strategy.

- Include elements of your brand story in your everyday client touchpoints including proposal documents, invoices, website contact page and emails.

- Weave your brand story into your bio and elevator pitch. The why is almost always more interesting than the what, and together they're a pretty compelling combo.

Business values and brand personality lie at the core of communications. It's one of the first questions I ask clients at the start of a new project and the two inform each other. If a business's values are grace, discipline and temperance, then it's highly unlikely to have a brand personality that is cheeky and irreverent.

As a communications specialist, one of my major goals while working with clients is to ensure their communications and brand story reflect their values.

Look objectively at your communications, specifically how they look from the outside. The goal is to ensure that branding remains unambiguous and your writing reflects the nuances and ethos of your business. Assess everything against your business values, from event promotion, blog posts, websites, email campaigns and social media. Are the messages confusing? Do they align with your business vision? Do they inspire or offend your target audiences?

Communications messages can either enhance or detract. They can support or demolish a brand. I love the part of my work that ensures writing remains bang on brand while hitting the right targets, confirming that the way a business looks on the outside matches its goals and values. Health and fitness businesses are often, unfortunately, and no doubt unintentionally, great examples of a disconnect between values and branding. They often have the values of empowerment, motivation, strength and community. Let's add welcoming, professional and inclusivity into the values mix. Step into the physical space of the business, and no doubt those values are on display via the staff, the equipment and the programming. However, dig a little deeper into their communications. Take a peek at their Facebook page or the blog posts on their website. I'll bet my bottom dollar that the content is at best male-centric, and at worst blatantly sexist. A lot of content I see is demeaning and irritating, and I'm not impartial to sending a quiet PM to businesses to clean up their posts and stop offending their broader audience. Good communications and a beautiful, evocative brand story can be achieved without a single flash of cleavage, or the suggestive use of a barbell.

CHAPTER FOUR

Reaching Your Target Audience

I'm no life coach, but I do know the feeling that comes with a lack of alignment between work and purpose, and it ain't fun. Many of us in small business start off accepting clients because we need to pay the bills and grow our business. Are they the right clients, though? Does the work fill you with dread or joy? Defining your target audience is a fantastic way to redesign your business and get you to a position where you work with people and businesses that fill – not deplete – your cup.

I often have clients who are highly aware that their communications lacks focus, and yes, that's a problem. If a mark hasn't been defined, then how do you hit it? Sometimes, people in service-based businesses (who I primarily work with) seem to fall into business with a client who lands in their lap without a lot of marketing work. Then the power of word of mouth and referrals keeps their business ticking along nicely.

However, for those who want more from our businesses than 'nicely', that's where powerful, strategic communications come in. But first, we need a defined audience to communicate to. If you're not talking to a specific someone, then who the hell are you talking to? The clearer you are about your audience, the more targeted (and clear) your messages will be.

Who are you talking to?

Ugh, surely not another communications Word Nerd bleating about writing a target audience avatar? Hells, no! As they say in the classics, and on my Facebook feed about seventy times a day, 'Ain't nobody got time for that!'

Look, I can't deny that I do a happy dance when a new writing client has extensive insights into the niche they work in. Having a clear understanding of your target audience or dream client is essential to beautiful, effective business writing. However, defining your client or audience can be right up there with a root canal. A ten-page dossier that would put ASIO to shame, which includes their audience's favourite Muppet character? Indulge me while I channel a post-Aussie Rules media interview: yeah, nah. That level of detail isn't necessary for effective communications. All you need, really, is just the basics and the facts, ma'am, just the facts.

If the business model is business to business, messaging and communications will be slightly different to the business-to-consumer model. However, the basics you should have in mind are:

- What is the business wanting to achieve?
- What are the pain points and problem areas?
- What are the services/products that can help this business achieve their goals?

This is, as I say, quite basic. The detail comes with further defining via your key communications messages. Outline how you solve your target audience's pain points quite specifically. The more deeply you understand your dream client's problems, the more you will have in terms of content to communicate how your solutions can resolve their issues. Your messages will write themselves.

Discovering/unveiling your target audience

The best (and quickest!) way to define your audience is to look at who you are already currently working with on your client list. What do these clients have in common? Where did they come from? Which/whom do you prefer working with? The clients you love will become the avatar of your target audience.

Another approach is to look at your services – specifically, the nitty-gritty about the benefits they bring to your clients. Now, who is in most need of that benefit? If you are a professional organiser, for example, and your time management brings a sense of calm and control to busy professional working mothers of school-aged children, then *boom*! You've just found your audience. Imagine you are a personal trainer specialising in fat loss for women over forty who are time poor. The messages that are going to target this audience will be completely different to those of a personal trainer who works with clients in their twenties who want to enter bodybuilding competitions.

Of course, demographics are important – if your services come with a big-ticket price tag, then there's not a lot of point wasting communications efforts targeting budget shoppers, to put it rather crudely. My point is not to lose hours of your working day creating a dossier of an imaginary client. It's more important to get a grasp of their motivations as this will dictate your messaging, while an understanding of who they are – i.e. who you are talking to – will inform your voice.

To niche or not to niche

I purposely avoid being a niche business because I love the diversity of my client base and, subsequently, the projects I work on. That said, I do have a very clear understanding of my audience in terms of my communications strategies and approaches and the voice I use for my business writing, and I have the same mentality when it comes to my client work.

Some businesses are concerned that if they niche too tightly – that if they write to that niche too deliberately – they'll exclude potential clients. But that's not necessarily the case. For example, I work with a fabulous executive coach who has the main audience of women in middle to senior management who want to take their career to new heights. She does work with men with the same aspirations, but she doesn't specifically market to men.

My experience, and I've been doing this shiz for quite some time now (#ohsoold) is that the message will reach clients outside your niche almost by default while hitting your intended recipient fair square in the you-know-what.

PART TWO

Let's Write Right

Holly Cardamone

CHAPTER FIVE

Writing Basics

Have you ever found yourself swept away by a beautifully written sales email, social media caption or website about page? Alternatively, have you found yourself completely turned off by really bad business writing with more than a touch of sleaze? Guess what? Me too! Let's go forth and craft copy that is beautiful, not cringeworthy.

There are five main sections to good business writing, which apply to what I see as the five essential elements of crafting an effective piece of business writing:

1. Planning a business writing project
2. Grammar and punctuation
3. Understanding the components of good business writing: house style, voice, point of view and structure
4. The actual process of writing
5. Editing and polishing

I've talked about what communications are and how to plan them. Now we'll explore how to write some brilliant copy.

The nuts and bolts of grammar and punctuation

When my older cherub started school, I was beyond excited to witness firsthand the magical process of a child learning to read. At the time, I was working part-time, and I was super keen to put my hand up to help in the classroom. Yep, one of *those* parents. Shhh ... listen carefully ... hear that helicopter? Before parents could be classroom helpers in the literacy program, there was a requirement that they attend a three-hour literacy program. Off I trotted, more than a little smug in my abilities. Here was I, a Word Nerd bookworm with Master level writing and literature qualifications, about to learn about how to support five-year-olds learning their magic words. I may have even scoffed. When the Deputy Principal/Head of Literacy asked who considered themselves good spellers, I shot my hand straight up in the air, then proceeded to misspell 'fulfil', 'daiquiri' and 'diarrhoea'. The last one was particularly discomforting, given my background as nurse and mother, i.e. someone who has interacted with more than their fair share of Code Brown situations. While my knowledge of where to stick an apostrophe remained secure (spoiler alert: not where you think), I had not even the slightest recollection of the difference between prepositions and clauses. It was a very humbling situation, particularly after my Smirky McSmirkface start to the session.

A super-quick refresh of grammatical terms

Verb (describes an action or state of being):
- She ***ran*** across the road.
- The cat ***was*** in the backyard.

Noun (describes a person, animal, object, emotion, place or concept):
- The ***farmer*** moved the ***cows*** into the ***barn***.
- ***Love*** of ***food*** is often called ***gastronomy***.

Pronoun (words that stand in for nouns):
- Holly got on ***her*** horse and rode ***it*** to the beach.
- The girls said ***they*** had taken the bag and tossed ***it*** over the fence.

Passive writing vs active writing:
- In active writing, the subject (noun) of the verb performs that action):
  Active: The cat sat on the mat.
- In passive writing, the subject (noun) receives the action expressed by the verb:
  Passive: The mat was sat on by the cat.

Preposition (words that introduce phrases):
e.g. at, in, on, over, under, above, beneath, into, onto, after, before, for or with.
- **After** the assembly, we returned to class.

Clause (includes a verb and its subject):
- Sally smacked the cat.

Sentence (contains at least one clause and ends with a full stop, question mark or exclamation mark):
- The banker counted the money.
- Did mother have dinner?
- That was a funny movie!

Adjective (modifies (describes) a noun):
- The school has a **bountiful** supply of **extra-curricular** activities.

Adverb (modifies a verb, adjective or another adverb):
- The school is **well** supplied with activities.
- Activities are **bountifully** available in the school.
- Activities are **quite bountifully** available in the school.

Ye olde dreaded apostrophe

No other type of punctuation seems to be such a PIA for people. I know some people get all angsty and uptight about using apostrophes – probably because grammar snobs like me get their (my) knickers so obviously and loudly in a twist – so they avoid them at all costs.

Here's the rule:

> **Apostrophes are used only to show possession or to indicate missing letters (contractions).**

Here's how to implement the rule:

> **Write the word that owns something, add an apostrophe, then add an s.**

- *Holly's dog is so adorable. I just want to squeeze that dog's cheeks.*
- *It's going to be a beautiful day. I'd like to go for a run, but I really don't want to, so I won't.*

Don't use apostrophes in:

- Possessive forms of pronouns – its, hers, ours, yours, whose
- Inanimate objects – the price of wool, NOT the wool's price
- Australian place names – Kings Cross
- Australian organisation titles – Workers Federation of Australia

How's that? Clear as mud? There are many resources available to help you brush up on grammar and punctuation rules. My one caveat? Make sure the ones you use meet Australian conventions.

Good business writing

House stylin'

As you may have guessed, I have a lifelong commitment to correcting the grammatical ills of the world, one sentence at a time. It's a blessing *and* a curse, and a cloak that weighs heavily, but is also worn with a suitable amount of pizazz. Ahem … where was I?

When working on a client's writing project, one of the first questions I ask in developing the project brief is whether they have a house or business style. A house style is basically a set of guidelines about the way the organisation or business presents their written work. This document is called a House Style Guide.

Any piece of work involves making choices. For most people, these are largely automatic and without much thought but aren't always grammatically correct. How on earth can you possibly remember all the rules for your business writing? Easy peasy – create a business style sheet that sets them out. This means you don't have to try to remember the choices you've made in your writing process; this is particularly important so words are correct and consistently spelled, such as copyedit or copy-edit, travelled or traveled, wordnerd or Word Nerd.

A business style document is a tool that documents the rules for writing. This simplifies the process of both writing and editing work, and ensures every document is consistently adhering to a preferred, agreed format.

The main elements a style document covers include:

- Formats for headings, lists of points and tables
- Styles of quotations (singular, always singular!)
- Placement of punctuation marks
- How to render times and dates
- Preferred versions or spelling of words that live in your style sheet, as above (programme vs program)
- Guidelines on non-discriminatory and gender-neutral language
- Preferred dictionary

Some clients do utilise a house style, but most don't. In those circumstances, I just apply my own based on the Australian *Style Manual*, also used by most government-funded departments and agencies and professional editors. Here are some of my style rules:

- Headings should be in title case: a mix of upper and lower case.
- Subheadings should only have capitals on the first word and any proper names.
- Paragraphs should be a minimum of three sentences. Try to avoid excessively long paragraphs and avoid single sentence paragraphs unless it's a design choice.
- Use consistent spelling based on the Macquarie dictionary, avoiding Americanised spelling:

- Our vs or (flavour vs flavor)
- Ise vs ize (organise vs organize)
- Exclamation marks convey excitement and urgency, but use them sparingly.
- Question marks should be limited to direct questions.

Voice and point of view

Have you ever met someone in real life who is a complete disconnect from their online or writing persona? It's decidedly disconcerting, even more disconcerting than my undying love of adverbs, if that's possible. Sometimes people who are warm, funny, approachable, accessible and engaging in real life come across as overly formal, stuffy, forced or contrived in writing, and vice versa. Why? They haven't nailed their voice.

Here's the thing: nailing voice is not easy. There was an entire study unit dedicated solely to voice in my Writing and Literature Master's in the context of narrative, non-fiction and fiction, because voice is one of the critical elements of readability. In terms of business writing, especially writing for small businesses, I don't think the importance of voice can be overstated. Why? Storytelling is such a fabulous way to have people engage with your brand and be more inclined to work with you. We know that people buy from people and/or brands they like and so your voice (or your brand's voice) should evoke both your likability, and the essence of your personality. The person in the email or in the social media caption should be a super close representation of what comes out of your mouth and your body language when you meet someone face to face. I know I'm doing my job well, and that I've nailed a client's voice, when I get personal messages to them via their social platforms, sometimes a little too personal!

Before writing anything, I know exactly how I want it to be received by the intended reader, and I use the voice and the point of view that is going to best connect. Voice isn't just what you say, but it's also how you say it. It needs to be a fit for your brand, and for your audience and includes language, expressions and turns of phrases.

- First person is perfect for anything personal. It's relatable, resonates and is engaging.

- Second person can be effective with copy that you want to speak directly to your client, such as sales copy.

- Third person adds some distance between 'you' and the subject and can be useful for projects that are information-based such as blog posts or articles, particularly those that are industry-specific.

Some quick tips to improve the expression of your voice:

Write like you speak

Writing for business isn't the same as writing university assignments with correct citations, hypotheses and an absence of contractions. Not many people say 'do not' in a sentence – unless it's directed to the offspring about to push a sibling into the swimming pool. Record yourself if you need to, and take note of the nuances in your expression.

That's your voice!

Read your work aloud

Before you hit publish on an email, a blog post or social media caption, quickly read it aloud. If it's clunky, or if you trip over words, your voice is out.

Be a fit for your audience

Voice isn't just what you say, but it's also how you say it, and like all communications, needs to be a fit for your brand, and for your audience. The language, expressions and turns of phrases you'd use if your brand was in the surfing industry targeting adolescents are completely different to that of a marriage celebrant targeting baby boomers celebrating love late(r) in life.

Channel your passion

Regardless of your industry and your target audience, nailing your voice is much, much easier when you have some passion and enthusiasm for the content you're sharing. If appropriate and not totes awks (as my ten-year-old says), record yourself talking to a friend about your content. For example, if the content is your website about page, tell your friend what it is you stand for, what you want to do within your business, and who you want to do it for. It's pretty hard to subdue your enthusiasm when discussing your work passion with a friend, and you'll end up with a ton of content for you to tweak, restructure and fiddle with to get your voice right within the context of your content. In fact, almost all of my writing projects with clients start with me asking a few pointed questions that open the floodgates.

Your brand's pronoun

In communications, brand voice is critical to connection. Voice is a reflection of brand personality and persona and influences the way a brand connects with an audience and vice versa. When working with a client on their communications, their voice is one of the first things I audit; and as a writer, pronouns are essential to voice. I know not everyone is grammar obsessed like moi (but oh, what a magical world that would be), so here's a quick refresh on a pronoun:

Pronoun: Words that stand in for nouns.

In terms of business communications and a brand pronoun, it relates to whether a brand (Company X) calls itself 'we' or 'I' within a sentence. It's a question that comes up all the time in my communications advising sessions with people who are sole traders. There's really no absolute answer.

My experience is a lot of businesses of one use the 'we' pronoun to be seen to be bigger than they actually are, and because they feel it adds an element of professionalism to their message. Personally, when I rebranded and launched Blue51 Communications, I used a 'we' pronoun for that reason, as I'd worked as in-house communications director and had worked with agencies who were firmly in the 'we' category. I felt like it was a necessity. With hindsight, I know (firsthand!) that the 'we's' were very much 'I's'.

Very few of us, despite what our ABN classification says, work in isolation. I'm a sole trader, but I work closely with other sole traders and companies (i.e. web developers, graphic designers, bookkeepers and accountants, virtual assistants). I'm a one-woman show, but strictly speaking, I don't run my show completely solo. Even so, it felt insincere and phoney to refer to my team, and more than a little pretentious.

I stuck with the 'we' pronoun for almost a year, but I discovered fairly quickly that the 'we' pronoun wasn't working in my favour. Firstly, everything I wrote (*everything*) felt arduous, difficult and inauthentic – because it felt misrepresentative. Secondly, my clients were coming largely via word of mouth and recommendation, and people wanted to work with me, Holly Cardamone, and not the business. The 'we' had to go. As soon as I shifted my message from 'we' to 'I', everything shifted. My writing flowed, my messaging was clear, and I felt a much less tenuous connection to my audience.

At the core, the audience should define the pronoun. Have a quick think about your audience: the people you want to work with. Do they need or want to identify personally with the person behind the brand? Do their needs (and your value proposition to meet those needs) require a personal, authentic connection and relatablity? Do they need to know, like and trust a brand as a person? Is your professional relationship with them based on personal connection?

I'm not big on acronyms other than WTF, which I tend to use on the daily, but it's worth thinking about your connection with your clients. Is it B2C (Business to Consumer)? B2B (Business to Business)? Even in the category of B2B, it can be further tightened to P2P – person to person. When you're one person speaking to another person, the pronoun can either make or break that connection. Using 'we' implies a group of people from your business is talking at that person. Using 'I' implies you are personally speaking directly to and with a person. Back to my experience – personal connection was key to my ideal audience relating to me and my work and taking that next step to investing in their communications with me as their Word Nerd. It also was (and is) a way to screen potential clients to unearth the good eggs I really want to work with and exclude those that I wouldn't be a good fit for.

If your business is focused on the personal, and you very much want to be a face behind your brand but you have a team, you're not completely restricted to the 'I' pronoun. Honesty and authenticity are important to brand reputation, and it's obvious when someone isn't forthcoming with how much they actually do in their business. Do you think Oprah does everything in her empire herself? Use messages such as 'my team and I', or 'I love what my team has created for ...' or 'my team has been ...' This is still first person but indicates you're not a solo operation/superhuman.

Your broader vision for your business also influences your pronoun. If you have plans to scale and expand and potentially sell your business, then the 'we' pronoun is completely appropriate. I have a number of clients who are currently solo but have plans to expand, so we've created a strong brand persona to enhance their personal feel and sense of connection and relatability in their messaging. We use (see?) language such as 'all of us at Company X are excited for', or 'the team caught up recently to talk about our ...' and the brand voice is fun and friendly to bring the audience along for the ride.

If you've been battling along in the world of 'we' but want to move across to 'I', a good way forward is to do a really strong introduction post on your social media platforms, or perhaps a blog post, saying 'this is who I am'. That draws a line in your communications sand, and frees you to move forward in the world of 'I'.

CHAPTER SIX

Structure

Writing projects have different structures, tied to purpose. What are you writing? A brief, an email and a social media caption will all have different structures from each other, as well as from a sales or event landing page. A media release follows the structure of a news story with a descending hierarchy – an upside-down pyramid – with the most important, newsworthy info at the top, then the less important, background information follows. A services page will have an almost inverse structure.

The beginning

'Where shall I begin, please your Majesty?' he asked.

'Begin at the beginning,' the King said, gravely, 'and then go on till you come to the end: then stop.'

– Alice's Adventures in Wonderland by Lewis Carroll

The beginning is the most important piece of the writing and is what makes a reader decide to keep on reading or to scroll on by. Consider how you want your readers to respond emotionally to your introduction: shocked, surprised, seduced, inspired, heard? There are seven main types of introductions:

1. Summary – brief synopsis of the key elements that will follow
2. Quote – statement from someone central to the content
3. Description – words that paint a picture
4. Anecdote – a little story relevant to the bigger story
5. Statement – using fact or opinion as the first sentence
6. Question – posing a question
7. Delay – suspending vital information to create tension and grab attention

Examples of introductions

- Summary: There are many hundreds of options for mortgages in Australia. Choosing the option that's just right for you isn't easy.

- Quote: 'Sean's knowledge and expertise are second to none. We know for a fact the rate he secured us was the best for our circumstances.'

- Description: Mortgage rates are enough to make a mild-mannered homeowner break into a sweat. There are just so many options, and the jargon that the lenders use makes it so much tougher to make a decision.

- Anecdote: Sally and John spent the good part of six months going from lender to lender, trying to find someone that spoke 'bank' and wasn't just giving them either the runaround or a take it or leave it, or a hard sell. That's the beauty of a mortgage broker – we do the running around for you, and we speak perfect 'bank'.

- Statement: There are over 999 home loan options available on the Australian market.

- Question: Did you know that 97% of homeowners don't feel confident that their mortgage is suited to their circumstances?

- Delay: Australian homeowners are at great risk – and they don't even know it.

The middle

You grab their attention with your beginning, but the middle is where you woo them. The middle paragraphs of content are where you might need to work to sustain your reader's attention. It's the substance, thus facts, texture, descriptions and opinions, and where you might address your client's pain points with story. Each paragraph needs to speak to their motivations – and yours!

The end

The end is also critical because it will direct the reader to your desired next steps, AKA the call to action. What is the feeling you want to convey at the end of the copy? What is the response you want to elicit? A call to action is a natural conclusion for your writing.

Five tips for a fantastic call to action

A call to action (CTA) is a non-negotiable for all communications activities. Why? Because it makes your ideal client's life easier by telling them explicitly what you need and want them to do as they engage with you and your business, and what the next steps are for moving forward.

1. Use a simple design for enhanced clarity. Don't have a truckload of options, and use lots of white space to make it easy for people to follow your intended actions. Want some examples from the best in business? Take a peek at the homepages of Google, Dropbox and Evernote.

2. Be clear about what to expect, indicating through concise copy exactly what will happen once a person 'subscribes,' 'downloads,' or 'clicks here,' with a focus on the benefit that person will experience.

3. Place a CTA on every touchpoint, including every page of your website. Don't ask people to consume a piece of you (a social media profile/bio, a blog post bio or a marketing flyer) without giving them logical next steps that are aligned to your business goals.

4. Use enticing, compelling copy with lots of action words and just that right amount of excitement, passion and a dash of spunk.

5. Don't overstep the mark. One of my pet hates is being asked for a ton of information that's not needed. For

your mailing list, it really shouldn't be more than a first name and an email address.

Wait, what about pop ups, I hear you wail? Personally, I can't stand them, I find them a visual assault and they fragment my experience online. I don't use them on my website. Having said that, they perform exceedingly well in conversion, so go with what suits you.

CHAPTER SEVEN

The First Draft

OK, OK, I know I've just bombarded you with a lot of information. I know that all these steps can feel a bit daunting to a novice copywriter, but they won't be after you've written more words. In fact, the more you write, the easier it becomes and the better the end result.

To get there, though, is to remember that everything you write should be considered your first draft. Your first draft is just a space to get your thoughts down – thoughts that later can be shaped into fabulous copy.

The concept of a first draft is to create before consuming. It's one of those things – the only way through it is to do it. You can't edit a blank page, so sit down, bang out your words, get that shiz written and then go back and edit. Don't tweak and fiddle during your first draft. Just keep moving forward, one word at a time.

The writing process for a first draft is very much playing with words and ideas, and having fun with it! Before you begin writing, stick that inner editor where the sun don't shine, as they say in the classics, or at our family get togethers. The point of a first draft is to just write.

You see, if your inner editor hangs around while you're writing, that first draft is much, much more difficult to write. Inner editors are annoying, distracting little fleas. They will tell you when you've misspelt something, they'll tell you when your punctuation is off. They'll tell you that your sentences are rubbish, that nothing you write makes any sense, that no-one likes you and you should just give up on the whole writing caper and just pay Holly to do it.

Thus, thy inner editor – bugger off, please!

Want a quick strategy?

You have your plan of what you want to write, how you'd like it to feel and how you'd like your reader to respond; now go forth and write! It's as easy and as hard as that.

Mac users will love the inbuilt Dictaphone feature. Yes – scribble out the outline of what you'd like included, and then talk into your Mac. Watch the words that pour out of your mouth transform into copy – sweet, sweet copy. Keep a close eye on how it's being transcribed because it's not perfect.

If you're better at conveying your message via voice or video – do that! Record yourself pretending to speak to your dream client, and then transcribe it into a Word document. This is a fabulous way to capture your passion and enthusiasm for your work and all the umms, arghhs and clunky expression will be cleaned up when you edit.

Holly Cardamone

CHAPTER EIGHT

Editing and Proofing

Good writers are often highly critical of their work. Imposter syndrome kicks in hard during the writing process. We've all seen that meme about the creative process being a journey from 'this is awesome' to 'this is shit' to 'this will do.' Sometimes, the writer is so close to their own work that they lack perspective. It's a great idea to create some distance between what you've written and the editing process – even a quick run around the block, or a break for lunch will give some perspective.

Got your perspective? Right, let's get to work!

Editing

My editing process is as follows:

- Read the entire piece in one sitting (if possible).
- Read all the headings and subheadings to check for accuracy and consistency.
- Read the paragraphs for consistency and logic of ideas.
- Read the individual sentences, looking for correct grammar, sentence structures, punctuation, spelling and word choice.

Some initial questions to ask with the first read-through:

- Does it flow in a logical, yet engaging way?
- Does it have the right focus?
- Does each paragraph add something new?
- Have you varied the sentence lengths?
- Is there any unnecessary repetition?
- Do you have an effective call to action?
- Is it clear what you want your reader to do with your information?
- Are the tone and language tight and appropriate for your audience?

Proofing

Before you hit 'go live' and dance around, high-fiving strangers, proof your work. Proofread it, then proofread it again a day later, go for a walk and proof it again. Give it to another set of eyes, as they'll pick up issues that you will have inadvertently skipped.

Proofreading checklist

Print your work and read it out loud. Always, always, ALWAYS send yourself a test email campaign before sending to your list, and even better, if you have your own Word Nerd (friend, colleague or mum), ask them to have a look. Then check the following:

For copy:

- There are no spelling mistakes, or grammar or punctuation errors.
- No words have dropped out.
- All sentences make sense.
- There is no potentially defamatory content.
- Your copyright is included across everything.
- Contact details listed are correct.
- Links are correct.
- Acronyms and abbreviations are spelt out in full with the acronym in brackets when first used, then acronyms used subsequently.
- Quotation marks used consistently.
- Subject lines are complete.

For structure:

- The words at the top of each page follow on from words at the bottom of the last page.
- Header/footer is correct throughout.
- The cover title and other details are correct with no typos.
- The quality of images is appropriate and correct.
- Colours and branding are aligned to visual style.
- Headings and subheadings listed in the contents page match the headings in the copy.
- There are no errors in the headings.
- Headings weight (font, size, colour) are correct and consistent.

CHAPTER EIGHT

Finished? Happy with what you've written? Now do that happy dance I mentioned earlier. Double points if you do it on social media and tag me so I can join in.

CHAPTER NINE

On Point Writing Habits

As someone who writes for both business and for fun, I've learned a few tricks and tips when it comes to establishing good writing habits and how to turn musings and scribbles on Post-its into strong communications.

Strategies and habits to adopt to improve your writing

Read like a mofo

Apologies if you were expecting something more eloquent, but writers read. They read voraciously across genres and they devour language. As you read, collect words and turns of phrase that tickle your fancy, such as '*tickle your fancy*,' and use them for inspiration.

Set writing goals

Like most areas of my life, I apply a goal process to get things moving, especially while writing. It might be a certain number of words a day (hello, NaNoWriMo!), or a project stage. Some people like the whole 'don't break the chain' concept, where each day of writing earns a red cross on the calendar, or set time-based goals such as writing for a certain time, or action-based goals such as publishing a weekly blog post.

Schedule

Make writing a priority, and set aside non-negotiable time in your workplan or schedule to tackle writing projects. If you can't squeeze a daily writing practice into your schedule, then aim for regular batch writing sessions, monthly or quarterly, which I find really productive.

Write without entanglement

By this I mean bang out your writing project, then go back and polish. One of my Writing and Literature Master's lecturers used to bellow 'you can't edit a blank page.' Alas, on reflection looking back, I'm pretty sure he lifted that from another great literary mind. However, it's true.

Banish fluff

Both in your writing but, more importantly, in your process. Don't sit at your desk, staring out the window, waiting for a muse to wander by, swinging her hips and showering you in a wave of inspiration. I honestly don't believe in writer's block – instead, I prepare against feeling blocked by having a ready supply of content ideas and post plans. Who has time to wait for inspiration to strike?

Lessons from NaNoWriMo for content marketing

November is the most magical time of the year for Word Nerds around the globe. Why? It's the annual 30 days of insanity that is NaNoWriMo. It's a strange acronym, which stands for National Novel Writing Month. The basic premise is to write 1666 words a day, every day, for thirty days, resulting in a novel of 50,000 words. I first discovered NaNo when I was doing my Writing and Literature Master's and fell in love with the concept straight away.

Here's what I love about NaNo in the context of content marketing and writing for business:

- It involves goal setting that is crystal clear, achievable and just a little bit nuts so as to involve growth and development.

- The concept is wholly focused on creating before consuming – it's easy enough to get stuck into 'research' with writing projects, but the only way to get something written is to write. #funnythat

- Again, you can't edit a blank page, so for 30 days, do nothing but bang out the daily word count and *then* go back and edit. Don't tweak and fiddle – just keep moving forward. This approach stops the over analysing and uber judgement.

- It pushes you firmly out of your comfort zone. Let me be clear – writing 1666 words a day isn't easy. Some days, the words flow, and my record is just over 11,000, which I don't recommend because my fingers swelled like sausages. However, on other days, the words just don't come, which of course means hitting the word count is really difficult. Once a day or so is missed, the word count becomes really daunting, extremely quickly.

- It is extreme, but it is doable, even if you stretch your goal by 12 weeks to decrease the word count to 500 words per day.

- The approach can be applied to any project within a business.

NaNo is basically productivity on steroids. I love that the urgency created with a 30-day goal makes me focused and moving forward towards the end game.

Writer's block be damned!

I don't believe in writer's block. If I waited for the muse to strike, then I'd never get anything done. Having said that, ideas don't always flow, but after being a working writer for such a long time, almost twenty years now (sheesh, how did that happen?), I have a few tricks up my sleeve for when I'm not feeling particularly inspired, but still need to churn out some words.

Writing prompts are much-loved tools in creative writing and journalling circles for good reason. They can help shift a writer's perspective and exercise the imagination muscles. In terms of business writing, they take what can be an angst-ridden process ('argh, what the hell do I write in my god-forsaken e-news welcome message this month?') into one that's much less resource and time intensive.

I use prompts in my own business and for my clients. They're my tried and true methods of getting words out of my head and onto the page, or screen – words that educate, words that convert, words that engage and words that sell! Below I have detailed some of my favourites, designed to inspire and to spark your imagination. You won't use all of them for all your writing projects – you might find that some are more suitable to a colloquial form of writing, such as social media posts, while some will help you write your blog posts, or your monthly e-newsletter. They're not meant to directly translate into content pieces; rather, use them as launchpads that could potentially generate an almost unending list of content ideas. You might be able to brainstorm a ton of content ideas from all of them, or you may find that one or two are the ones you find the most useful and become your go-to; either way, have fun with them!

Here are some prompts to use to gather ideas to feed your content marketing strategy:

FFS, oops I mean FAQ

What is it that time and time again you get asked about in terms of your work or your industry? What is it you wished you were asked about your work? Take ten minutes (seriously, put on an egg timer) and scribble down all the questions you can think of that come up in your client meetings, your enquiries and in your general conversations with people about your work. Turn each of these into a beautiful piece of content.

Old school mind maps

Confession – I love a mind map, and a lot of writers do. They're a great way to plot out anything from a series of poems (#wildchild), a novel, or to plan and execute interviews. Try a mind map of your service offerings to imagine what their titles could conjure in the minds of your clients. Put each main service offering you have in the centre of a sheet of paper and use them as spark words to create ideas of topics that could become blog posts, fact sheets or articles you could send to your mailing list.

Look within

Within your Google Analytics, I mean. There's a wealth of data there for you to mine for your content writing plan of attack. What search terms are leading people to your website? Are these the terms you're expecting? Let them inspire you, and brainstorm content against each.

Get help

If you're feeling well and truly stumped, or completely uninspired, then go to a tool like Buzzsumo to get you moving. Chuck in your preferred keywords, and out shall spew forth a ton of content topics that perform well in your niche.

Improve your writing by learning from others

Before writing your own projects for your business, it's a great idea to have a think about what you believe makes writing 'good' (for example: interesting, easy to read, motivates you to take action) and what makes business writing 'bad' (boring, dense, infuriating). You do this via reading, reading and more reading.

Another method is to learn from others by creating a Swipe File. It is a technique copywriters and journalists use to apply proven formulas and techniques for drafting copy. For someone in business, creating a Swipe File is a fantastic way to create a repository of fantastic writing techniques and strategies to apply in your own business. A Swipe File is not for blatant copying or plagiarising. It is research: a way to understand how to apply techniques and ideas.

Here's what I collect:

- Subject lines and headlines
- Blog post introductions
- Event marketing
- Graphics I like
- Calls to action
- Opt-ins
- Landing pages
- Stuff-up corrections

PART THREE

Stories in Action

Holly Cardamone

CHAPTER TEN

Tell Your Story With a Bloody Good Website

Creating your online home for your business – AKA your website – is such a fantastic, fun project. It's where you share all your plans, dreams and schemes for your business. However, there's no denying that it is a big job. It's time and resource intensive, and it's easy to miss some details in the execution.

Before we get stuck into the essentials for an awesome website, I need to point out that my focus is not technical or SEO, but rather communications, branding and messaging. There are some key essentials that every website should include, that are easy enough for a non-tech-head to implement.

Copy

Essentials are your contact details (and make sure they're correct!), calls to action that are aligned to your business purpose, social proof, information about what it is you do and how people can work with you, social sharing buttons, opt-in offers to build your list, copyright, privacy policy and terms of conditions. Most important of all content is your about page.

Branding

Your website is the online home of your business, and thus needs to be an accurate and positive reflection of your brand. Use a style guide that details your structural formats (headers, copy, lists of points), your design elements (fonts and sizes) and preferred tone and voice.

SEO features

There are copywriters who specialise in SEO (and a whole lot of spammers), however, I personally have had really good results using a plugin called Yoast SEO. You write your copy, your titles and metadata, and there's a little traffic light at the base of the page that tells you quite clearly how your page will perform and gives detailed information about how to improve.

Analytics

Measuring your site's performance is essential, but there's a ton of information on Google Analytics. I suggest picking a couple of important metrics that tell the most comprehensive story and sticking with them for analysis.

About page gold

Many people tell me that their existing about pages just don't sit right. Putting the spotlight on yourself is hard, y'all. You have a story to tell but every time you start to bang it out, all you think is, 'Oh Lord, how boring am I?' It's like when you were twelve, hearing your voice on tape and vowing NEVER to speak again. It's really difficult to write about yourself objectively.

The about page is the most important page on your website – no debate. It's where you introduce yourself and your business to the world. Statistically speaking, it's also the most viewed page on a website. You have two to five paragraphs to tell all and sundry who you are, what you do, and how you do it. You know you're much more awesome than those 200 words sitting there trying to entice people to your business. Your about page needs to be professional yet personal, fun and creative, clever but not cutesy. Add compelling, welcoming and memorable to that mix. It's a delicate balance to get right and it starts with a simple yet deeply complex question: Who art thou?

People like to know who they're dealing with; the human behind the brand, if you will. The most critical element when it comes to writing an about page is your audience. Keep your target audience in mind before you draft as much as a dot point. Your audience will determine your tone – are you chatty, conservative, technical or colloquial?

Ingredients to include in your about page

Headline

Of course, 'About' or 'About Us' or 'Who' is the standard, but depending on your industry, you can add a little more creativity if you so desire. You have my permission to go wild with maybe even a 'My Story'.

Name and profile of key staff

This is where your bio sits and is a chance to show yourself in your multifaceted glory, and give your visitors a glimpse into the person behind the business that extends beyond the job title.

What you do

This is slightly different to your services page, but given about pages are usually navigated to within two clicks, it pays to list them here, clarifying your business and the services you provide in a couple of sentences.

Your experience

Don't rattle off your CV. Instead, tell a story about who you are professionally, including your work history and education. Use your skills, education and experience to fill the blanks within the context of a story. It's not an easy balance, but it's doable.

Photo

Go on, smile, my precious. Or stare off into the distance pensively, or stroke a hairless cat while looking mischievous. You choose.

Call to action

Create an opportunity to continue the conversation. The easiest, no muss no fuss way to do this is to include a call to action that links to your social channels.

The other important thing to note is this type of content is never static and should be constantly tweaked and updated.

Beautiful bios

About pages are an opportunity to turn your CV into a story by taking your skills, experience and expertise and crafting them into a narrative. A bio is the extension (or is it contraction?) of this. Given the multitude of places it's used, it's the perfect place to slap a ton of personality into what can often be a bland piece of business writing.

A bio, when well written, establishes trust and tells a much bigger (and better) story than your CV ever could hope to. Basically, a bio will reconcile your skills, education and experience within a personal narrative. Storytelling, am I right?

Like any other element of your business writing, your bio is a communications tactic that enforces and enhances your brand. It's a way for people to fall in love with you at best, or relate to you at least. It's a quick and easy way to establish trust, and it can make the much bigger story of your CV more accessible. It frames a conversation, sets a tone, and when well-written, entices and compels. A bio should tell a story.

The best bios tell a story through compelling, personal and personality-filled copy. My goal in crafting bios is to frame the content as a conversation. I want to set a tone that is non-didactic but expresses passion, that is enticing, authentic and accurate. I aim for less of a resume and more of a story about a professional and personal journey (#soz). I usually write content that answers five basic questions:

- Who am I?
- How can I help you?
- What's my back story?
- Why can you trust me?
- What do we have in common?

Bio therapy

I find that most people need a few different variations of their bio to meet different purposes. Case in point – your Facebook bio will be different to your LinkedIn profile summary. There should be three specific bios at a minimum for your communications toolkit:

1. Basic first-person, elevator pitch.
2. First- or third-person paragraph (5–10 lines) for guest blog posts, speaking notes or other introductions.
3. Long-form bio with extra detail and a call to action.

All three need the principles of story to create a connection. Share a blend of personal and business information to paint a picture of the person in 3D. Some beautifully applied writerly glitter will turn your bio into a story without adding buzzwords (bleugh) and with clarity and concision. The voice (first or third person) will depend on the audience and the purpose of the bio, so is interchangeable.

Here's an example of a slightly more irreverant bio for a less formal audience and purpose:

Holly Cardamone is a communications advisor and writer from Melbourne, Australia. When Holly's not consulting with businesses large and small to provide communications support, writing fabulous copy for her clients or creating strategic communications plans to support their business goals, you'll probably find her at the gym alternating between burpees, ball slams and cursing, or trying not to drop her iPhone as she takes countless photos of water in her eternal quest to capture the perfect shade of blue. She's a mama, a wife, a Word Nerd and the person you want on your table at a trivia night.

SEO, optimisation and grammar brutalisation

Look, I'm certainly no SEO-pert, but if you want to be found online, then there are certain steps we must take. Every time I speak with someone about their business writing, Google and SEO rears their (ugly) heads. Let me be clear: I write to an audience, not Google. Everything I write is tied to broader business goals and a target audience, both of which direct messages. That said, of course you want to be found on Google. Why else would you put any time, effort or dosh into an online home for your business? Your content needs to be easily found by your audience, and Google will help in that process immeasurably.

Without a decent sprinkle of Search Engine Optimisation (SEO) throughout your site – using keywords specific to your business and industry – your beautiful website is just not going to be found.

Here's what NOT to do:

> *Each Blue51 Communications morning starts with a Blue51 Communications meditation specifically designed for Blue51 Communications by Blue51 Communications to Blue51 Communications the bejesus out of the Blue51 Communications working day.*

There's more to SEO copywriting than repeating (and repeating, and repeating) a set of keywords. SEO is a science and, done well, an art form. It is extensive, detailed and dynamic, multifaceted and complex. The bare bones, however, is matching your content to what people, your people, are looking for online.

Before writing as much as a headline, have a quick think about your dream reader/client, specifically in terms of the work you do for them, or the services you'd like to be providing. This will make it easier for you to imagine the search terms your clients are banging into Google to find a business just like yours, that solves the problem they are facing. It can be difficult to retain objectivity when writing about something close to you, and sometimes we need a reminder that our industry jargon isn't always used by our clients. Knowing the terms that your ideal client is using – or having an awareness of these – is essential to optimise your content. You might find it useful to make an ever-growing list of these as you're thinking about it, and add to it as you come up with ideas, phrases and words.

Here are some of the less colourful search terms that have led their way to me (Blue51 Communications) online:

- Writer in Melbourne for annual report
- Bootcamp blog writer
- Business writing Melbourne
- How to be a freelancer
- I want to be a freelance writer

Armed with your keywords and search terms, craft or tweak your content, incorporating your keywords as you write. It's easy to see when a website has been written for SEO – it's jarring and the content doesn't flow. A little bit of creativity, some careful structuring and forethought to content, and this shouldn't be an issue. Perhaps use your keywords in your headings and subheadings, and then write your content in alignment.

As I said, SEO is a science and an art form, and maybe even a bit of a headache.

Let's assume you've:

- Created a list of terms (or keywords); and

- You've applied them across your page titles, image captions and subheadings appropriately and thoughtfully.

Now, go forth and create content with SEO and your specific keywords front of mind:

- Using your dream client's language, create keyword-focused theme pages in the form of blog posts with baity titles – videos if that's your thing, FAQ pages again, specific (keyword) topics, and link your relevant content.

- 'How To,' 'Five Ways To' and 'Three Steps To'-type headers are SEO effective and also easy to promote across social media platforms.

- Encourage links pointing back to your site by guest blog posting and listing on (appropriate!) business directories to move your website from essentially an online brochure to an information source that is dynamic and evolving.

Finally, measure, measure, measure, and then adjust your content accordingly. That's the best thing about internet communications – you haven't forked out $100k for a television campaign. Everything you do can be manipulated, changed and improved upon.

Lovely links

You've done a ton of keyword research. Yes, you've sprinkled your copy with said keywords. Yes, you've optimised the F out of your PDFs. Here's another strategy for you:

Links.

Many moons ago, when I started my Communications Master's, the internet was new, less than five years old. I heard the expression, world wide web, and that's exactly what it is: pages of content linked together to form a web. My first impression of the www was how perfectly suited it was to poetry, moving text not just down a page, but through a page. Yep, I was that cool.

Fast forward almost two decades and it turns out links aren't just good for poetic Word Nerds, but search engines actively reward linking algorithmically. And yes, that's a real word; I checked.

Links, both external to your website and internal, are essential to SEO because the search engines leverage the quality and quantity of links to determine how sites relate to each other in terms of popularity and authority. Websites that have earned link authority and popularity over time (e.g. *The Huffington Post*) will bestow competitive ranking to another site that it links to.

There are also some other benefits to incorporating linking into your website and content schedule:

- Linking to resources and content that your ideal client will benefit from or enjoy extends your value beyond your website and social media presence. This means you are not simply a one-way source of information but a contributor and a participator.

- Links within your website are essential not just for SEO but for your ongoing brand awareness and promotion. You have pages and posts of content on your website – link to them so your audience is clear about who you are and what you do.

- Guest posting provides not only the opportunity to insert at least one link back to your own website, but will give you access to a new, complementary audience.

Links are lovely. They move your website from a digital brochure to an information source, a web, if you like, that is dynamic and evolving, and the search engine gods shall reward thee.

Entice people to your website

Do you have a beautiful website? Have you created an online space where people want to hang out, linger, move from space to fabulous space? Do you have a fantastic user experience that allows your visitors to seamlessly and effortlessly learn more about you and your work, with navigation that is intuitive, simple, logical and helps people find what they're looking for?

User experience blah-blah aside, sometimes people just like a bit of a guided tour. Here are some ways to virtually hold someone's hand, and gently, yet emphatically yank them around all the pages you so lovingly built on your website.

Facebook

Facebook has lots of opportunities to send people to specific pages on your website. What's your social media strategy? Is it to regularly showcase your people, your services or products, or to provide answers to those questions about your business that you're asked time and time again? Providing direct links to specific pages with good captioning is a great way to move people around your website pages. Another opportunity is to take advantage of Facebook's About and Services sections to provide links to pages you wish to drive traffic to.

Instagram

Instagram is more limited than Facebook in that the one linkable space is within the bio – so make it work for you and for your business. I love using Linktr.ee for this purpose, but you can just as easily use a (hidden) page on your website. Your link is the call to action of your Instagram account, so have it directing people to the number one place you'd like them to land, based on your business goal. Is it to build your list? Have it directed to your landing page. Is it to share a recent blog post? Put your blog's home page as number one. You get the drift.

New enquiries

I have quite an elaborate proposal document which I provide to people requesting quotes on my services. I include the all-important dollars and cents, but I also give people an overview of me, and of Blue51 Communications. Depending on the service requested, I often provide links to case study posts of similar projects, and I include links to my testimonials page.

Onboarding new clients

Once a client accepts my proposal and has paid a deposit to get cracking, I provide them with a welcome kit that outlines expectations for working together and confirms deliverables, but again I use this as an opportunity to take people for a tour of my website.

Landing pages and mailing list welcome confirmations

People have expressed an interest in your work by signing up to your mailing list, so the logical next step is for them to be guided around your website. Include the pages that are most relevant, such as blog posts connected to the opt-in they've signed up for, information about working with you or the pages that share the content that your happy clients have provided about you and how ah-ma-zing you are.

Calls to action

Every single page of your website, including each blog post, is an opportunity to direct people around your website.

Look, I'm not in the business of sugar-coating (I wish!), so I can't say that creating a website is a quick and easy communications tactic that you can knock over painlessly or effortlessly. It's a big job, no doubt about it. However, as your virtual storefront, your digital home, it's one of the most important touchpoints people will engage with, so let's make it every bit as lovely as you are, shall we?

CHAPTER ELEVEN

It's all About the Content

Gorgeous content marketing

Content marketing, am I right? It's so hot right now, and no doubt the main biz advice screeching at you in your social media feeds is telling you to get your content out there in the world, and tout sweet!

Guess what – the hype is true. Digital marketing, with a strong content focus, is undeniably powerful in terms of brand awareness, thought leadership and turning leads into clients. However, like any communications, it needs to be strategic and aligned with your brand and your business goals. Don't go throwing out blog posts or podcasts for the sake of it – give your content marketing a bit of love and a bit of strategy.

Wait, you want me to give away my hard-won IP via content marketing? Are you mad? No, I'm strategic, and a bit of a potty mouth, but mostly strategic. Every now and then an article pops up claiming that sharing free content is a dead strategy, that it's a waste of valuable time and energy and has very little benefit to a business's bottom line. As a communications specialist, a writer for business and someone who works in digital communications and marketing every day – ERRY SINGLE DAY, I tells ya – I wholeheartedly say, 'Nay.' #buggeroffnaysayers

It's a rare communications plan of mine that doesn't include content marketing as part of an overarching communications strategy. When content – useful, helpful, beautiful content – is sprinkled out into the world like alphabet confetti, the benefits are tangible and measurable (my favourite) with a return on investment – AKA ROI ASAP, WTF, OK I'll stop now – so significant that giving up isn't an option.

Content marketing is exactly that – the use of content to share your expertise and showcase your knowledge, skills and experience. Content marketing is the ideal way to communicate with your ideal client to share your story and to promote your work; to use your voice to show them that you 'get' them, and allow them to 'get' you. When you create and share helpful, useful and entertaining content that answers your ideal client's questions and frustrations, it positions you as an expert. Implemented consistently, you'll be front of mind when they think, 'Now, who is the expert when it comes to …'

Content can be text or copy based (i.e. blogging, social media captions, white papers, ebooks, etc.), video, visual graphics, charts, infographics, hell, even your elevator pitch could be considered content marketing. Of course, as a writer, blogging is the medium that lights me up most of all.

Blog to build your brand

Blogging is a freaking fabulous communications tactic that I simply adore. Why? Let me count the ways:

- It's a way to build brand awareness.
- It's a way to establish your credibility as an expert.
- It rewards you with Google love.
- It feeds your social media schedule.
- It gives you a reason to write!

Blogging is an effective online marketing tool, and one I believe almost every business could use and have fantastic results. It keeps the Google gods happy with all that delicious fresh content driving traffic to your website. Blogging also offers a really powerful call to action opportunity. Yes, you have a contact us page, but there's something much more compelling about a well-written case study blog post. It also provides a means of encouraging people to join your list or work with you. AKA – 'Want to know more? Join my mailing list and receive my pearls of wisdom direct to your inbox!'

The other thing I love about blogging is the way it melds so beautifully into almost all communications tactics, but it's especially resourceful when it comes to your social media content calendar. Do you ever scratch your head for content ideas to post on your social media platforms? Share your blog posts, share excerpts or fab quotes from your blog posts, and get your followers excited about what's coming up next in your blogging schedule. Another bonus? Readers can share your posts (either direct from your website or your social media channels) with their followers, and boom – there's a gazillion extra eyes on your website.

Want to know my favourite reason of all? Hands on heart, what I love best about the medium of blogging is it gives you a chance to write. Just as sleep begets sleep (or so I'm told), writing begets writing. The best way – and the only way – to become a better writer is to write. Writing is a critical skill for any business. Think about the amount of writing you do on any given day, even emails, and all of these written forms of communication reflect upon you as a person and as a business. Get it write – oops, I mean right!

Content marketing planning made simple

I work with a lot of people who see the value in blogging for their business, but just can't make it happen. Some people simply can't find anything to write about, which can happen when we're too close to something. Others are overflowing with content ideas, to the point where it becomes overwhelming, or where they blog about everything and anything but their writing isn't aligned to their communications or broader business goals. This is where you need to look at pillars.

Content pillars guide your content marketing plan and should be complementary to your broader business goals, as well as your communications goals (refer chapter one).

Is your reason for blogging to share your expertise? If so, then this will inform your pillar – for example, I have two content pillars within my plan that share my knowledge and experience: Communications Toolkit and Writing for Business. They share very specific information and tips and tricks against those two categories. Some of my writing clients have pillars aligned to their broader business vision, for example, Women in Leadership, Fit Family Food, Gender Issues and Manage Your Time, Manage Your Life. Your pillars may not be something you ever outwardly identify; rather, they remain an internal guiding structure. Sometimes, they inform and guide the development of a content marketing plan, and at other times they reveal themselves through a brainstorming session.

I can't deny it – content marketing can be a beast of a tactic. It's a beast that needs to be tamed, and tamed *hard*. So, how does one go from having ideas scribbled on Post-its – or from no ideas, zero, nada, zilch – to a full content plan with beautiful, evocative, cohesive pillars? It all happens with some good old-fashioned Word Nerd sorcery and some basic organisation skills. Shall we dive right in?

It all starts with a bucketful of ideas. There are two approaches to generate ideas: the first is a wild brainstorm using great writing prompts, including those shared in chapter nine. I have fabulous, tried and tested writing prompts that I've used for over twenty years for my own business and for clients which I'm more than happy to share – just reach out via the contact details at the end of this book. The second approach is to brainstorm slightly less wildly against your content themes or pillars. Once your bucket is overflowing, sort each individual idea into categories. Some will be obvious – for example, if you're in the business of counselling women leaders, and you have an idea for a post about equal pay, then you would allocate this to a category that focuses on gender issues. As the themes emerge, think very clearly about your business goals and what you want to be known for as you narrow your pillars into distinct categories – six at the very most.

Once allocated to a theme or pillar, it's time to decide on your blogging frequency. For over five years, I've blogged with a four-pillar content plan published weekly, because maths hurt my head. Each week in the month could have a different pillar. Easy peasy! Monthly is absolutely A-OK, too. Consistency is key to successful content marketing and fitness and parenting and pretty much everything, really!

Now all that's left to do is schedule each post weekly, fortnightly, monthly or quarterly into your content or editorial calendar. This is basically a planning tool, and a way to organise your:

• Key topics of information
• Posts that provide content against these
• Dates for publishing the content

I'd love to tell you to open a spreadsheet, set some categories and formulas, or download some fancy-pants app, but that's a big fat lie. Get thyself a monthly, quarterly and yearly planner. There are lots of great templates online, or maybe even start with a big piece of paper, or to make it feel super lovely, go to a beautiful Swedish-inspired stationery store, you know the one, and buy yourself a gorgeous monthly planner. Insert into your planners all the essential dates for both your business and your personal life. Include launches, events, new product or service development and releases, anniversaries and marketing projects. Basically, enter all of the milestones you're anticipating. It's important to include external days, such as formal holidays, as well as random quirky holidays that suit your business, such as Talk Like a Pirate Day – seriously, who doesn't love that one? Although, my personal all-time favourite is Word Nerd Day.

From here, depending on your frequency, physically allocate each Post-it/blog post idea into the relevant pillar in the relevant week or month. Yes, you heard it here first, I'm telling you it's perfectly OK to scribble out your content plan, for an entire year if need be, by hand on a physical piece of paper. Of course, if you're a spreadsheety type, you can then transfer this into whatever electronic form you like, but bottom line? You'll know exactly what you are going to write about for the time ahead, removing any chance of writer's block. Of course, if needed, you can move topics around to suit what is happening with your business and the outside world, but the framework remains the same.

Finally, include a process for the process:

- Research
- Write
- Edit
- Publish
- Create social media posts to promote it
- Schedule promotion within social media calendar

Gah, that's a lot of content when talking content, I get that. The most important thing to keep in mind with all this is to remember why you're using content marketing in your communications in the first place. Yes, it will build your credibility, but more importantly, when done well, and done strategically, it will give your audience something they're looking for, and provide a solution for what ails them. No biggie.

That's how we tame an unruly, slightly aggressive content marketing beast – now, off you go and write!

Case study your way to communications gold

Gosh, I love a case study as a communications tactic! I think case studies are under-utilised, possibly because so many of us drowned in churning out academic case studies for university, which were often dry and boring. However, when written beautifully (but of course!) and used strategically, they can be a powerful tool.

Here are the key benefits of including case studies in your communications:

1. They describe a problem or an issue and how you as an expert solved it.
2. They help establish your credibility and authority.
3. They promote your business and your expertise, so you become the go-to.

Want to know how best to use your case studies in your communications beyond your content strategy?

Sprinkle them like glitter:

- On your website
- On your testimonials page
- In your pitch, proposal and quote documents
- In your media pitches
- Verbally at meetings and events

Guest blogging

Providing guest blog posts for other businesses is a fantastic tactic for online marketing and to promote your own business. Guest blogging is a way to expand your audience and increase your online presence. If building your email list is a goal (and it really should be), guest blogging gives a unique opportunity to encourage a new (to you) audience to join your adventures via your email list. Include a clear call to action that directs readers to 'find out more' about you with links to your social media platforms and your sign-up page. It allows you to build your brand, as well as the perception that you are a person who knows their stuff when it comes to your speciality. By sharing your ideas, thoughts and views on your specific niche, you become known as a go-to person. The other benefit is the love Google will send your way with quality inbound and outbound links.

Now, there are some words of caution I feel obliged to include:

It's essential that if you are providing content, you are proud to be aligned with the site or the business! The blog and blogger need to have an audience that complements yours, or one you would like to have. Also, be clear that their brand values match yours. Take a look through their social channels – especially Instagram stories – to be clear that you're a perfect fit.

Guest posting is such a great way for a freelancer or emerging business to get their name out there – and the social networking benefits which I haven't really touched on are the extra sprinkle on the cupcake, or in some cases (including mine), the ginger in the green smoothie.

My guide to content ladders

A content ladder is a fabulous tactic to embrace. It's a way to take something and maximise its impact across multiple touchpoints and audiences. One piece of content can be turned into so many things. Imagine you're a naturopath and you've written a blog post about the importance of sleep. Your blog post listing ten facts about sleep could be turned into:

- An online graphic representing the ten facts.
- An infographic for Pinterest, Facebook and email campaigns.
- Ten individual social media posts for Facebook, Instagram and LinkedIn.
- Ten individual social media videos for Facebook and Instagram.
- Responses to media call outs.
- Footnotes in corporate emails, invoices and receipts.
- Email campaigns to prospects to reiterate the value of your service.
- FAQ page content.
- Ten individual blog posts that detail each fact in greater depth.
- Ten individual case study blog posts highlighting an individual fact.
- Ten individual videos or Facebook lives that detail each fact.

Clearly, this is enough content to fill a schedule for months, if not years. I know I'm a Word Nerd, but this concept gets me positively giddy with the possibilities.

Ebooks

Ebooks are fantastic tools in your content marketing and lead generation toolkit, which often don't require a ton of additional work. If you blog regularly and have been for some time, with some quick tweaks and writerly glitter, you can turn that content into a product you can use for a multitude of purposes.

Pick a topic or subject for your ebook, one that is reflective of your area of expertise, your goal and purpose for the project and, of course, tied to your audience's interests, motivations and problems.

Be sure your content is logical, coherent and follows a straightforward path. Consider creating an outline or an overview first, detailing what you'd like to include, the detail and the benefits. Keep in mind that this is an ebook, and you don't have to cram all of your knowledge, thoughts and insights into it. You can always write more! If your outline is looking too big, with too many concepts, split the content into different ebooks.

While your ebook isn't supposed to be a another *War and Peace* (we're talking anything from three to fifty pages, not fifty thousand), like any writing project, your copy should be engaging, compelling and clear.

Include gorgeous design in your budget, and while there are programs like Canva that make design easier, an actual, real live, breathing, walking, designing graphic designer is completely worth the dollar spend. Put it this way – spend hours dicking around doing it yourself, as well as the writing, as well as the promoting, as well as running your business and working with clients OR handball it to a designer who will make good use of your copy and content structure in a visual format.

Create a compelling call to action that aligns tightly to the goal for the ebook project. Give readers something manageable and inspiring to do with the content or give them something to make them want more of you! Be clear about the process of accessing the ebook – does your audience receive it in exchange for their email address? Is it part of a broader communications strategy? Hint – if I'm your Word Nerd, then yes, it is.

Edit your ebook like an … editor! Or get someone else to go over your work if you feel too close to it. At the very least, print it out and go over your content with a pen first, with your outline (if you created one) nearby to keep the bigger perspective in view while you're deep in the detail of chapters, paragraphs and sentences.

Make the most of the medium and hyperlink the crapola out of your ebook. Have links to your website, to specific pages within your website, to your social media handles, etc.

Don't forget the basics – introduce yourself! Don't assume that because someone has accessed your ebook that they know who you are, what you do and how they could work with you.

Curate and create

Content marketing is a massive time suck. There, I said it. It's not a quick and easy process – well, not if your plan is based on quality. Writing is really the quick part – there's also researching, publishing, sharing, repurposing, lions, tigers, bears, oh my!

What if there was a way you could have a robust, comprehensive, kick-arse content strategy that doesn't involve you writing each and every part of it? The answer, my pretty, is content curation, and it's a little somethin' somethin' that always brings a sparkle to the eye of my communications clients.

Here's the thing – not everything you share in your content marketing strategy has to be yours. Nor should it be. Now, isn't that liberating?

Curating content gives your audience access to a variety of voices – not just yours. Sharing content from other sources shows a level of generosity and that you value difference. It's a holistic approach to your content strategy and, from another perspective, is one that relieves hours upon hours from your workload. It's a value-add for your audience that is relatively simple to implement from your end.

Curating content can position you as an expert in your space, as it gives you the opportunity to add your own perspective, position and viewpoint to what you're sharing in your caption. Pose questions, challenge assumptions and have a conversation with your audience in that context, particularly on LinkedIn, which has the core purpose of being a forum for professional exchange rather than general chitchat.

The content you share needs to be aligned to both your business purpose and message and to your audience's needs and interests. Create categories that your audience will appreciate and resonate with, and that are a natural fit for your business pillars and branding. For example, my audience is primarily people with their own service-based business. The topics of interest to them (and me) inform the basis of my content curation pillars, so I share a lot of content about productivity, good (business) reads, writing tips and tricks and communications. After defining your topics, then find content that follows that topic. There's fantastic content from sources such as Flipboard and Medium, as well as from the people, brands and businesses of people you admire.

There are many tools for sharing curated content, but I like to keep things super simple. As I find content beneficial to my audience, I copy the URL to my notes app. When I'm ready to share curated content, it's a simple copy and paste, along with a pithy caption.

Curated content is helpful marketing at its very best, with your audience's core needs (inspirational, informational, educational, motivational) at the heart of your strategy. But one last comment – do it properly and ethically! Attribute, don't steal, and link back directly to the original source.

Holly Cardamone

PART FOUR

Spreading the Word

CHAPTER TWELVE

Email Marketing and List Building

Why build a list?

Remember the days of dial-up internet, when the only sound better than that screechy connection whine was the ping of a new email? With upwards of 100 emails hitting my inbox each day (and that's after regular massive cull and unsubscribe sessions), I don't really experience that thrill of excitement with each new email. In fact, more often than not, I turn off notifications when I need to buckle down and get sh*t done. However, don't listen to anyone who says email is dead. There's no doubt that email is powerful, and very much still a dominating channel – the conversion rate for email is still way above other online channels when executed beautifully. Best of all? Email isn't a slave to a reach algorithm – your message lands directly in someone's inbox, not hidden away in a feed. This is why the mailing list is the temple at which we worship.

Social media is a non-negotiable, must-have communications strategy for 98.9% of businesses, no doubt about it. However, there's no escaping the fact that the lack of control of a channel is problematic. So many people I know (including me) have fought the urge to shed tears of pure frustration because of the impact of the latest algorithm on engagement. It's not a great idea to have social media as a sole channel of communicating with a target audience; your communications need to be implemented alongside broader, complementary strategies. Put simply, it's a good idea to gently shepherd people off Facebook and onto your mailing list.

Clients are sometimes reluctant to add 'create, develop and nurture the bejesus out of a mailing list' to their overflowing list of things to do in their business. Strategically managed, a list will drive people back to your website, help you remain front of mind for your zone of genius, and engage your target audience in a personal, meaningful way.

The people on your mailing list (when they're gained legally and with no icky practices like signing people up without their consent) have shown a genuine interest in your business. It makes absolute sense to stay in regular contact with them. But how, how, how? Easy peasy lemon squeezy!

Emails are awesome. They're one of the most effective ways for a business to communicate with their clients, and to market and brand themselves and build a loyal following. I love email campaigns, and I often recommend them. There are right and wrong ways, however. Want to alienate your hard-earned email list and breach countless international privacy laws at the same moment? Send an email to your clients, all 477 of them, with their email addresses visible to each other. Seriously, nothing annoys me more than seeing my name alongside a whole lot of others in a group email.

Hello, Creepy Gary, you tall, lanky, slightly wild-eyed bloke at my gym who makes awkward small talk about the size of my 'weights'. I'm so thrilled you have my personal email address. Not his real name, of course. I'm all about respecting privacy. But Gary, if you're reading this, a nod is fine. It's the gym. I'm not there to chat.

There's an easy way around the potential of breaching privacy. Use one of the many, quality email marketing platforms. There are many reasons why:

- Unlike email sent from your email system (mail, Outlook, whatever floats your boat), you have access to invaluable insights. You can see how many of your recipients actually opened your email, who they are and which subject lines they respond best to. You can also see how many recipients are unsubscribing.

- Make notes against your mailing list and create segments for targeted campaigns. There's not a lot of point in sending Gary a discount voucher to your post-pregnancy Pilates workshop.

- The sign-up process and forms meet Australian privacy and spam legislation. This is important to the goody-two-shoes out there like me.

- Design, design, design! The leading generators have interfaces that make it easy to slap in your logo and branding, add images to your emails and hyperlink the hell out of your text, making your email something your recipients want to read and are more likely to forward.

You can code if you wanna (#showoff), but you don't need to.

- Setting up an automated email sequence to nurture new subscribers is a quick and easy process. It's a way to implement a well-considered communications strategy to build relationships, trust and education – content marketing at its finest.

Email content

Delivery mechanics aside, obviously, the content of your email is critical. There are a few tricks to writing effective emails that people want to open and read, that motivate readers to follow a call to action:

- Consider the call to action and then work backwards from there. Clarify the ultimate goal for this campaign/email and its specific purpose. This insight will direct the call to action.

- Write in the voice of a human and, as much as possible, and wherever appropriate, keep the tone conversational and one-to-one.

- Personalise, personalise, personalise as much as humanly possible. I love a 'Hi Holly!' I'm not so fond of a 'Hi First Name Surname!'

- In terms of language, use the word 'you' rather than 'I' or the product to help a reader connect with the copy and make it relevant to them as an individual.

- Closely align the goal with the reader's motivation, considering the ways a reader could benefit from the offering.

- Related to the point above is the subject header – this needs to be catchy, appealing and aligned to both the reader's motivation and the client's goals. A simple 'we want you back' reminds a client you exist, and that you've provided a service in the past.

- Finally, ask for the close (i.e. the goal) and ensure it is easy for the reader to respond with a simple 'click here'.

You had me at hello … That's it! A quick and easy guide to drafting an email campaign.

The anatomy of a gorgeous landing page

A landing page (or three) is essential for an effective list-building strategy. Strike that – landing pages are essential for many communications and online marketing tactics because they're specifically created for an action – in this case, to sign up to a list.

Some people use their home page as a landing page. This isn't ideal as a strategy because it's just a smidge too open ended. Your home page is your front door; a landing page is the servant's entry where you want the baker to deliver the bread. You don't want the baker wandering through your house dropping crumbs everywhere, do you? Basically, a landing page controls how people land on your site and the action they take once they're in your online 'hood and require clear and direct messages with very little ambiguity – actually, make that none at all. Banish all hints of ambiguity to the pits of hell, ploise!

A landing page isn't the place for a *Lord of the Rings*-esque rumination.

All you need is:

- A headline
- A subhead or tagline with a hint of suggestion
- A brief description – so brief it could be worn by an 'influencer'
- An image
- Maybe (and only maybe) some social proof by way of a testimonial

There's a trend I'm seeing for massive, long-form landing pages, which I know is based on a US online marketing tactic. I've been asked to quote on landing pages where an outline of inclusions would make the copy in excess of 5000 words. I can write these, and do, but my question to clients is always based on the audience. Will their audience of time-poor working mothers sit and read 5000 words? If yes, I'll happily write; if not, let's cut the waffle and get straight to the good stuff.

Some people also like to include a video within landing pages – I'm personally not a fan, but again, the specified audience is the driver behind content like this. If they'll watch it, go ahead and include it! But keep in mind the goal of a landing page, which is usually to solicit a response. Let's make that an easy solicitation, shall we?

Has your mailing list lost that lovin' feeling?

So, your business has one hell of a mailing list, created and curated carefully over time through networking events, through opt-ins, through beautifully designed and executed strategies. Initially, you gave lots of thought and love to your list. You created an email communications strategy – aligned to your business's broader communications strategic direction, of course – complete with timeline and a schedule of email campaigns that included what you intended to say to your list, what you wanted them to know about you, about your services. You were hellbent in your mission to provide useful, helpful content full of value-adds to give your list an insight into working with you, to share your knowledge, and dare I say it, inspire and engage.

The first couple of months went well; you met your deadlines, your content went out to your list consistently and then … and then … You skipped a scheduled mail out because you were busy with client work, or a project completely took over your work schedule. One deadline slipped, then another, and then another, and suddenly you realised you hadn't sent anything to your list for yonkers. Now it just feels awkward, and you don't know how to reconnect with your list, or how the recipients will react when you land back in their inbox.

You know what? The impact on your business when you neglect your mailing list isn't great. Email marketing is a fantastic business communications tool because it's a way to build relationships and connection, share an insight into working with you, or a way to keep front of mind. However, a neglected list is not a dead strategy and the end of email marketing for your business. We can fix this situation and get back on track.

Create a quick content plan to see you through three months, six months or even a year of monthly emails. Emails can be in the form of a newsletter, a letter from you, or a curated list of your blog posts, special offers, or behind-the-scenes information. Basically, have the content outlined as much as possible to make it easy for you to bang out email communications even when frantically busy. Keep the focus on getting reacquainted with your business, and adding value and benefits rather than lead generating – don't ignore someone for six months and then hit them up for a sale!

Reach out to your list with an email full of brand personality and a heartfelt apology for your absence. If appropriate, explain what's kept you from their inbox and reaffirm your commitment to regular communications with them.

Now, meet your commitment! Send out emails to the schedule that you promised with the associated content that you outlined.

Another thing you can try is a quick Facebook campaign, with some lives and some posts expressing your commitment to your mailing list, what subscribers can expect and maybe even an inexpensive ad campaign that targets your mailing list. You might get new subscribers who don't want to miss out on your fabulous content, and your existing list will have a double touchpoint.

CHAPTER THIRTEEN

Entering the Social Media Labyrinth

Which social media platform is right for you? Almost every business knows they need a social media presence – that's a given. They need it for brand recognition, to drive traffic to their website and/or their bricks-and-mortar store, and as the foundation of their content marketing strategy. The how, the what and the which isn't quite so clear.

While it's important to secure your online real estate, don't scatter yourself across all platforms willy-nilly. Nay. What I suggest is you register your business handle across them all, then pick one or two platforms to focus on for the next three to six months, get to know them really well, post consistently, build your community within that platform, and then add another if you feel you can manage it in your work schedule.

But which platform is best suited to your business? Pinterest? Twitter? Facebook? LinkedIn? Instagram? All of the above?

I'm always banging on about target audiences. Who are they? What do you want them to know about your business? Where are they hanging out? That's because knowing your audience and marketing and communicating directly to them, strategically and thoughtfully, is the most effective way to get ROI. What's the point of putting a ton of work into Instagram if your clients simply don't use it?

The clearest way to determine the right platform for you is to consider the following questions:

1. Who is my client/audience?
2. What interests them?
3. What is their platform of choice?
4. What do they use the platform for?
5. How will I meet their needs on that platform?
6. How can my message add value to them in their day-to-day personal and working lives?
7. Why do I want to engage with them beyond the almighty dollar?
8. What results do I expect from engaging with them?

If those eight questions are overwhelming, let's narrow them down to three:

1. Who is my ideal client?
2. Where are they hanging out online?
3. What content can I provide to them that will help me meet my business goals?

The answers to these questions will determine both the channel(s) you focus on and the content you share via that channel. It's not impossible for a business to be across all the channels, which is why Social Media Manager is an established job title, even though my parents have no idea what that means; however, for a number of businesses and organisations, it's unrealistic, and quite frankly unnecessary.

How to put the social in social media

Hey, guess what? Social media is a communications tool for connection! Can you believe it? It's not a one-way street. It's important to remain focused on not just selling, but engaging from time to time, too.

It's a (relatively) easy way for people (AKA your potential clients) to connect with you, your business and your brand and discover over time who you are and what your superpowers are. It is simply one more communications tool in your arsenal and needs to be used effectively to help, not hinder.

Social media is fantastic for brand recognition and for driving traffic to other sources (i.e. website and/or a bricks-and-mortar store front). Your business social media platforms are essential to your content marketing strategy; however, the core goals are community and engagement. Solely posting sales pitches to followers does not build a community, nor create meaningful engagement.

A key to social media success is consistency – you have to show up to be seen. I'm not saying NEVER include sales content in your feed, but limit it. There's a formula floating around the internet somewhere about 80% useful content, 20% sales, but that's all a little too Year 10 Maths for me. *shudders involuntarily* An easier proposition to adapt is if you post five or six times a week, then only one of those posts has a direct sales proposition. This entails being strategic and organised with a content strategy.

In terms of content, social media is all about building community and engagement – not constantly ramming key messages and sales pitches at your audience. However, social media is a communications tool, and like any communications tool, it needs to be aligned strategically to your brand and your business. For the love of all that is holy, please, please, please keep your posts on brand. Taking this one step further, no matter who your audience is, Neanderthal or otherwise, do not post sexist, racist or homophobic images, under any circumstance. Just don't.

Engagement and engaging with content is a way to send love and positivity out into the world, and that's never a bad thing. Social media engagement is a way to create a long-term relationship with clients and customers, and, of course, with your colleagues and supporters. The more engagement a specific post has by way of likes and comments, the better the visibility will be, rewarding it by the algorithm.

Share content – both yours and that of others, following, of course, correct accrediting etiquette – that your followers and ideal client will enjoy.

Respond to the content your followers and the people you follow share. Don't be stingy with your double taps, and allocate time in your schedule and workflow to go beyond the double tap and comment with thought and consideration. If someone has given you a real live LOL, tell them so! If their post reminds you of a conversation you had recently with a friend, tag that friend. If they're expressing that they're having a good time in biz, a hard time juggling the load or an absolute sh*tfight of a time, then acknowledge them and offer empathy.

Answer the questions people post on your platforms and the Facebook groups you are in. Bonus tip – keep a note of these because they'll feed your content plan. Don't forget to respond to comments. Engagement like this builds brand awareness and loyalty, but more importantly, connection.

Yep, social media is what the name implies; a two-way, somewhat real-time interaction. It's a medium that's unparalleled for building ongoing relationships from afar, or from across town, and is a beautiful way to tell your story, and you know how I feel about that, don't you?

Social media management in action

As a Word Nerd, the content creation involved in social media makes my heart beat just a smidge faster.

✓ I allocate a chunk of time in my weekly or monthly workflow to plan, create content and schedule the following week or month's social media.

✓ I sit down, bang it out, and check I'm not over or under posting sales content.

✓ I use auto-scheduling tools to schedule my posts for a week or a month.

✓ I can't stress this enough: engagement is essential to success. Twice a day, I jump on to the platforms and respond to comments, return likes when appropriate (avoid obvious spam accounts) and share other people's content. Twice a day is my goal in terms of productivity, but depending on the day, I will jump on and off a whole lot more, especially during school assembly.

Shhh ...

Generate a buzz on the cheap

Have an urgent issue to be addressed? About to release a fabulous new website/service/product/event/something? Have a massive launch coming up and you want to make the right communications calls to really generate a buzz and get your ideal client connecting with your business? Have a budget that's actually not really something you could, in all honesty, call a budget?

Your best friend in this circumstance is social media! While the Instagram and Facebook algorithms aren't as generous as they used to be, they're both still powerful platforms for getting your business in front of your ideal client. Even without committing to a Facebook ad campaign (which you could absolutely explore, and get good results for your spend), there are a few tips and tricks you could use to generate a buzz online with very little spend other than your blood, sweat, tears and creativity.

Write a clear and clever social media strategy for the project that's aligned to your broader social media strategy. Create a set of gorgeous content for the above, including sneak peeks, teasers and molto enthusiasm and excitement. Use a scheduling tool to ensure your content is going out at the right times and is consistent. Boom!

Is your dream client in a Facebook group?

Q: What communications strategy is best for your business?

A: One that will help you reach your business goals.

Q: What's the best way to use communications to reach your ideal audience so you reach your business goals?

A: Wherever they are hanging out!

More than one billion people are using Facebook groups, so there's a good chance that your ideal client is there, too. Hey, you're on Facebook more than you should be; might as well make it part of your communications strategy, am I right?

I really love Facebook groups as a business communications strategy and am a member of several. There are some really good ones, and some equally bad ones. The groups I love may have crossed my path by way of a value-add from a challenge, a purchase or a course, or they were recommended to me. There's almost a tangible sense of community, of people coming together online to share ideas, support, encouragement and motivation.

Benefits of joining Facebook groups

Find out what's hot and what's not

Have an idea for your business but not sure if it will stick? Trying to decide between directions for a strategy or process? Bounce it around your favourite group and get feedback from lots of different people.

Connection and community

Sometimes, having a business is professionally lonely. Facebook groups can offer a virtual community, complete with shared purpose and vision, and, depending on your business, your ideal audience. Connection is powerful, and my experience is the people in my favourite groups share generously with support and encouragement.

Sharing your expertise in a non-salesy way

Positioning yourself as a thought leader and go-to person for your niche is made simple in a forum that's based on providing support and information. When people ask questions or raise their business issues within the group that relate to your zone of genius – answer them! Be helpful, professional and provide simple solutions. Don't go nuts and give away all your IP, but it's usually completely appropriate to offer people the option of sending you a PM or an email for more information. You can also share tips or blog posts to groups with specific threads that call for such content.

Three quick tips:

1. Read the group rules and abide by them – AKA don't be a dick!

2. Respond to promo threads as directed – refer to point one above.

3. Make sure you make it easy for people to find out about your work by linking your business page to your about page in your personal profile.

Fix a stuff up with email

Mistake. Error. Stuff up. Oopsie. We've all experienced that immediate blood rush as we've hit send on an email we shouldn't have, or when someone has left a negative online post, or when a client has been unhappy. It feels awful – personally and professionally – even if it's as minimal as forgetting to add links within an online marketing campaign.

Corporations have entire PR departments on hand to manage their 'oops' moments, and some do it better than others (hello, 7/11 and your monumental pay nightmare). For example, recently, my telecommunications provider's mobile network went down, and soon after, they sent an email to their customer list with a very simple subject line – 'We're sorry.' They acknowledged the impact of the outage on their customers, detailed how they intended to mitigate the risk of the network being disrupted again, and offered free mobile data for customers for 24 hours. A PR nightmare was transformed into a PR success story in one beautifully written email.

Some errors can seem like a disastrous nightmare while in the heat of the moment. You can alleviate the angst:

- Simply breathe. Stop what you're doing, step away from your keyboard – hell, step away from your workplace, and just breathe. Calm yo-self.

- Respond relatively quickly but not immediately. Acknowledge the issue even if you don't have an answer or a solution. Don't be silent – let your clients or followers know that you're aware of the issue, that you're onto it and that you will keep them informed.

- Name the issue by identifying the problem, what's causing it and how you're fixing it. Honesty is always a good policy – but don't go into excessive detail. Apologise sincerely – indicate you are sorry for the impact of the mistake upon the individual. If it is appropriate or possible, offer a form of compensation, such as a refund or partial refund, a free product/service or an upgrade to their existing relationship with you.

Have some perspective and know that you can't please everyone. Some people cannot and will not be placated, despite your assurances. Move on. You've acknowledged the issue, you've apologised, you may have made an offer of compensation, you've done all you can. As TayTay says, shake it off, and get on with your day – having put in place processes to minimise the chance of the issue arising again, of course.

Avoiding and managing a sh*tstorm

A horrible side effect of the democratisation of the internet is the fact that anyone with access to a keyboard and wifi can leave nasty and unjustified public comments against businesses, more often than not with some fairly decent factual inaccuracies (AKA around 17 kilos worth of BS). It feels bloody awful, to put it mildly, and the first reaction is to want to click a finger and make it disappear.

There are some clear ways to avoid a sh*tstorm/stand up for yourself/respond to negative feedback in a public forum:

Reveal, don't conceal

Respond to the comment in the same forum. Don't ignore it. Hit reply, and acknowledge the comment, and acknowledge the concern and what you intend to do about it (see next point).

Go private

Try to take the conversation offline by writing something along the lines of 'Hi {insert name}, thank you for reaching out. Please contact us directly on {insert email address} so we can get this situation sorted out.' Don't engage in a public back-and-forth dialogue, but be authentic, helpful and human in your response, not (really) for the sake of the reviewer, but for the sake of the other people who may come across this interaction in the future.

Go into corpse pose for just a (mindful) moment

Or whatever it is you need to do to get your blood down from a rolling boil to a gentle simmer. Never respond beyond an acknowledgement or seek further details in an online response while you're feeling fired up.

Fact correct

If appropriate, and if the person continues to denigrate your business, reiterate your request for them to contact you privately while correcting some facts, politely and professionally. You might write, 'Thanks, {insert name}, as I initially responded, please contact me via email as I'm keen to have this situation addressed. According to our records/staff, the situation was {describe situation in polar opposite of review}.' Do it in a way that is respectful, yet clear to other people reading so they can see the situation for what it is. Engage only once, and as a person to reinforce the fact that you are a business that is caring, responsive and measured.

Completely out of line?

Check the review host's (Facebook, Google, Yelp, etc.) site rules to see if the review breaches them. If the review is completely out of line, is false or inappropriate, or includes profanity, threats of violence, racism or sexism, then request the review be removed on the grounds of breaching rules of use.

Embrace the silver lining

You may find that your other clients will see the reviews and jump to your defence, flooding your Facebook page with beautiful comments and five-star reviews. The negative review also may give you some insight or perspective into tightening up some of your processes moving forward.

Yep, a negative review in a public forum can feel like a whole bucket of poo raining down upon you, but a few deep breaths and a calm, professional and measured response will set things straight again. That and a few choice F-bombs that you share solely with your biz bestie.

Holly Cardamone

CHAPTER FOURTEEN

Hot or Not?

Social proof – what is it?

Years ago, I interviewed a business owner for a profile piece who had built an extremely profitable business providing educational experiences to small children. She had built a significant client base without a marketing budget, before these heady days of social media. How? Purely and simply, word of mouth.

Here's the thing, and feel free to quote me: mums in the park are a force to be reckoned with.

Basically, word-of-mouth marketing is getting people to do your marketing for you, and it can be really influential. It's hardly new; people have always shared their experiences with businesses, good and bad. When I started work in the communications sector, the buzzword for validation-based decision making was 'The Bandwagon Effect'. That shows you my age. Thankfully, I've stepped away from this slightly inflammatory term, and I now use the term 'social proof' to describe the phenomenon of basically wanting what she has – yes, that's it! From *When Harry Met Sally*, which is in my top ten of all-time least favourite movies, which also gives away my age.

At its core, social proof is word-of-mouth marketing, but the sheer scale of the online environment, and social media in particular, makes capitalising on social proof an effective brand elevator.

Are you your industry's best-kept secret?

It's not uncommon for new businesses to find themselves in a state of anonymity. Low social proof can have a massive impact on how you and your work is perceived, so social proof is a communications tactic that is a worthy inclusion in your toolkit. It plays a massive role in people's decision-making processes because it builds trust and credibility to validate decisions to buy from you or use your services.

Are you making it easy for your clients to toot your trumpet on your behalf?

Some simple tweaks and adjustments to your online and business communications could make all the difference in enhancing your social proof. Good social proof starts with giving service or a client experience that is so exemplary that people can't help but sing your praises. It must be respectful, values based and client or customer focused. It encourages loyalty, trust and engagement. It's being clear on your client's pain points and problems, and having a solution that addresses them, and addresses them in such a way that they feel compelled to share their experience with you with their friends and family, ideally for storytelling purposes with the same pain points.

Ask your existing network for referrals

This can be as simple as a 'tell all your friends' message at the end of a transaction, or you could put some more work (and writerly love!) into the process by writing a considered email, detailing the kind of clients you would like to be referred to, and asking if they know of anyone who would be a great fit. I know some people like to incentivise and formalise their referral process with a percentage of sales income, but at the very least a beautiful thank you card with a gift is always appreciated.

Directly request testimonials and reviews

Client testimonials are a fantastic way to provide validation of your work. Ratings and reviews are an under-utilised tool for businesses. We go online to research everything from holidays to haircuts. Encourage your clients to leave Google reviews at the very least, and if you have a review site specific to your industry, include these, too. Send a request for a testimonial and a review as soon as possible after a project completes. Make the process super quick and easy for your clients. Add the direct link to your Google My Business review page, your Facebook page and your LinkedIn profile. Maybe ask your clients to complete a quick questionnaire/survey to glean feedback and information that you can then rewrite into a testimonial.

Use your existing clients' experiences to create social proof content

Yes, I'm talking about case studies, but depending on the nature of your work and your branding, I don't mean university-esque case studies with citations and executive summaries and all that jazz. Case studies take people step by step through the process of working with you, as well as the final results that your clients have experienced. Basically, your content can show the problem your client has faced, your approach for addressing it, and the glory that rained down upon them post working with you. Highlight and showcase your work with clients and the results you've achieved, and while you're at it, share your clients' logos on your website and your social media schedule.

Highlight your 'as seen in' content

Have you been interviewed by a journo? Have you guest blogged for someone? Been a podcast guest? Any media mentions? Share details about your awards, interviews, profiles, publications and achievements across your website and social media platforms.

Put your followers to work

Social media makes it insanely easy to build social proof – it also makes it easy to fake it, but that's a discussion for another day, requiring a whole lot more coffee. A simple way to implement a user-generated campaign is to simply encourage your followers to use a hashtag specific and unique to your business while referring to your work in your feed, either for the purpose of a competition or simply just to be part of your community.

So, where to put all this delicious social proof?

Well, anywhere and everywhere! Don't be stingy; sprinkle that shiz like confetti! Include it on your landing pages, in your email campaigns and your social media schedule. Build a dedicated, testimonial-only page as a personal brag page, and link to this in your email signature. Include testimonials in your proposals and quotes, in your new client welcome kits and in your speaking engagements. Toot that horn!

We are the champions ...

There are many, many tools for promoting a business, but if the business is one in which humans – real living, breathing people – are the focus, then champions should be a core element of a communications campaign. There are many definitions of champions in the marketing world, but my definition is centred on having a recipient of a service or product as the 'face' of the communications, or the hero in a story. I love using champions in business communications, and in many cases, the participation of the direct beneficiaries in promoting the business is imperative to the success of the campaign. Seriously, who better to promote a personal trainer than the person rocking out the gun show?

Here's why:

- They become an advocate for the business, and not just a client.

- In promoting your business, they encourage and inspire others to join them.

- They reflect your brand and your business.

- They represent your ideal client, and thus people (also your ideal client) can identify with them.

- They showcase your business.

- They support and add validity to your business.

A champion-based social proof campaign is ridiculously fun to put together, but it's also beautifully affirming. Who doesn't love hearing nice things about themselves? You can use your champions to promote your work and to help you tell your story through interviews and profile pieces online, in publications, at events and in your digital strategy. Guide them (nicely and delicately) to focus on the benefits and rewards they experience through working with you, promoting the impact of how you simply improve people's lives through your skills, expertise and experience.

Tell me more – nail that elevator pitch

When you work for yourself, and/or when you are just starting out in business, a rapid-fire way to grow your client list is to network, network and network some more. If you go to networking events (oh, the humanity), you get very familiar very quickly with the concept of the elevator pitch.

Ugh … the elevator pitch. Along with school lunches, it's one of life's painful necessities. The basic premise is that you have 30 seconds to convey your business without boring someone's pants off. You need to be able to quickly and effortlessly communicate the values and benefits of your work in a way that is compelling, enticing and perhaps a smidge sexy.

When you're working for yo'self, you need to take advantage of all the opportunities to promote your business that can pop up as often as twenty times a day: at the school gate, at the gym, at the shops or even when you're bailed up by the eccentric person at your local train station. OK, picture this, you're at a networking event/bar/kids' sporting commitment, and someone sidles up to you and says, 'So, what do you do?'

If you're following all the advice in the business blogs, then you'll have your elevator pitch ready to roll. The theory is you should have a pre-prepared statement that explains what you do and who you work with in less than thirty seconds. Tell me that doesn't have disaster written all over it?

> *'Well, Barry, I'm glad you asked. I help disruptive, pre-menopausal women reclaim their authentic essentialism through wholehearted amplification.'*

Gah. Elevator pitches are often robotic and clunky, and as painful to deliver as they are to receive. Let's change that, shall we? Add some positivity and enthusiasm into your response, and speak as if you are a human, talking to another human – which, if you're reading this book, you clearly are.

Your description about your work or your business shouldn't be a conglomeration of as many verbs and on-trend adjectives that you can stick in one paragraph. Avoid the lofty generalities as much as possible, and instead, find interesting details in what you do. This will promote a two-way conversation by giving your recipient a curiosity pique rather than an ear bashing. I have a client who is a relationships counsellor and an accredited social worker, but that's not the basis of her pitch:

> *'I teach couples the skills to make a good relationship even better, and get a struggling one back on track. It's actually easier than you think to create an amazing, fulfilling relationship.'*

The unavoidable response to a pitch like this is intrigue:

> *'What's that? You teach couples the skills to fight less and have more lovin'? Tell me more …'*

And, therefore, the conversation continues.

No-one likes to feel unprepared and caught off the hop, so it's good to have a spiel about your work in your mind. As a writer, it's a pretty cool project to find a way to pitch your business in a clear, concise and consistent manner, yet feel engaging and interesting. The key is not having something fall out of your mouth that sounds rehearsed, mechanical, and, God forbid, poorly written. It's not easy to rattle off a line without it sounding forced or contrived. While it helps if a brilliant writer and communications specialist (who, me?) injects a ton of warmth and personality into it, unless you're an amazing actor, it can be hard to deliver your pitch convincingly and naturally.

I'm no actor, but here's what works for me when I'm asked what I do:

> *'I'm a communications specialist and a writer and I absolutely love what I do – I get to shine a light on people's work, so I help them create strategies, I come up with the messages that their clients will resonate with, and I give them a step-by-step way to make sure the right people are getting the right message. Easy peasy!'*

Or a variation thereof.

Basically, if you're passionate about what you do, and have enthusiasm for your work, share that passion and enthusiasm in the context of your results, and your pitch will sound fresh and enticing every time.

A word on feedback – the gorgeous, the average and the truly god-awful

Data from clients (AKA feedback) is essential. It helps people in business refine and create services, products and content that people can connect with, and stay on top of their clients' direct needs. Basically, feedback from clients is your litmus test for your business's performance, and when it's great feedback that indicates the value that you've provided, it gives a wonderful warm and fuzzy. Warm and fuzzies aside, I really love that feedback can be a strong marketing tool when used for social proof. Here are three ideas for easy extraction from your clients:

Online survey

Surveys are easy to set up, cheap (or free) and can or should be super painless for people to complete. Keep your survey short with no more than a handful of questions that take less than five minutes. Throw in some open-ended questions because that's where you'll find the storytelling gold. Ask questions that you need answers to, and those that lend themselves to beautiful testimonials. For example, 'How did you enjoy the experience of working with me?' and 'Would you recommend my services to your family and friends?'

Pick up the phone, or put your fingers on the keyboard

Directly seek information and feedback from your clients. Reach out to your clients, take them out for a coffee and request feedback in the context of improving your services and your client experience.

Leap through open doors

Often, at project conclusion, a client will send me an email that's relatively gushing with appreciation. I pounce upon these, and immediately hit reply and request permission to use their beautifully kind words as a testimonial.

Finally, be clear about what you'll do with the information received and that you'll be seeking permission to use the content provided in different forms across your social media, website and other marketing tools. Now go sprinkle that sh*t everywhere!

CHAPTER FIFTEEN

Expanding Your Client Base

Stairway to brand exposure – heaven or hell with fluorescent lighting

Ah, trade expos. Calves throbbing from twelve hours of standing on concrete, eyes bloodshot from the unrelenting glare of fluorescent lights, temple veins throbbing in tune to the neighbouring stand's bass-heavy soundtrack, jawbones fused into a permanent smile that's less welcoming and more manic as the hours (seemingly never) pass by.

Have you ever been to a fitness and health industry expo as a visitor, rather than exhibitor? It's such a fertile learning ground for communications because you'll see the good, the bad and the frankly perplexing. You'll sample some protein shakes, eat raw balls (do a hashtag search, and this will make a whole lot more sense), and you'll have flyer after flyer unceremoniously shoved at you by bored, unengaged promo people.

Trade expos, I've done a few, too many to mention (mumbled to the tune of 'My Way', for those of you playing at home).

While they are undoubtedly bloody hard work – please excuse my French, but I am Australian after all, and 'bloody' is central to our national vernacular – they can also be an effective way of meeting business objectives, be it raising brand awareness, gaining clients or selling.

Are they an effective way to showcase your business? Should you include them in your communications toolkit? Potentially yes, potentially no.

Attend expos that attract your target audience

Expos are expensive, and numerous, so choose wisely. Is your sole reason for being in business to provide vegans with natural, preservative-free protein supplements? The local salami festival is not your best bet for connecting with your target audience.

Be clear about your objectives for participating

Are you there to inform, educate, recruit or sell? This will inform or dictate the presentation of your stand, the messages you deliver and the materials and information you provide. This clearly relates to point one above – ensure every piece of information, be it verbal, written in flyers or your use of promotional items, has strong key messages that are strongly aligned to your target audience and your objectives for the expo.

Smile, don't snarl

Be open and welcoming, but not overly pushy. Seek eye

contact, smile, say hello, and then pause. This allows visitors to look beyond you to your stall, and make an assessment on whether to engage with you (see below). If they show interest, then respond, perhaps by asking them about how you/your business could be of assistance. If your number one goal is to grow your database, then make it easy for both yourself and for attendees and automate as much as possible using iPads – these make it quick and easy for you to get people's details. I much prefer quickly typing in my details than completing a hard-copy form – it doesn't help that those tiny little lines never fit my scrawl.

Make your stand somewhere people want to be

If possible, configure your stand in a U shape. A table across the entry of the stand with the host sitting behind it suggests: 'Keep walking, you're not welcome.' If said host is scrolling through a phone or has their head down reading a book, the suggestion then escalates to: 'I am completely and utterly disinterested in you so for the love of God, keep walking, don't even pause.'

If a U configuration isn't possible, then push your table right to the back (dressed beautifully, may I add, with a floor-length table cloth as a bare minimum), and stand in the entrance to your booth, to the side, so you're not blocking your styling, with a smile on your face and your phone away. Call me grandma if you must.

Your stand is a reflection of your business and brand, and it should appear as such, again, reinforcing the key messages that apply to that specific target audience at the expo.

Aesthetics are quite personal; however, the most effective stands are those that aren't overly cluttered but look professional, interesting and give a clear indication of the business or brand. Your logo and a tagline that defines you should be above eye height, so it's easily spotted across a sea of people, but without masses of images and slabs of text.

In terms of providing promotional materials, it's no surprise that popular stands are those with a whole lot of free crap, but be strategic and use materials that attract your target audience and will live long beyond the expo, with your logo and URL front and centre. Inflatable toys will attract kids, but they'll also annoy their parents. Lollies are eternally grab-able, as are pens and notepads. Personally, I'm an eco-warrior and so I avoid anything single-use.

Follow up, follow up, follow up

Of course, this may not be relevant depending on your objectives for participating in an expo, but if your goal was to connect and engage and you managed to get a stack of business cards, then get on the phone or email once back in your office, and touch base. If you collected names for your newsletter list, add them to your database, and send out a quick email to these newbies welcoming them to your community (yes, awful word, I know, but it's applicable, so I'm using it) and let them know they'll receive your next newsletter shortly.

That's it: my quick and dirty guide to having a successful presence at a trade expo. Enjoy!

Social butterfly time

I do love a soiree, I can't deny it. Can't, and shan't. Almost all events are fun and exciting, but launches are perhaps my favourite. Launches are (usually) the celebration of a long-term goal met, and a reward for late nights, early mornings, stress, excitement, IT headaches, and basically the sheer tenacity and perseverance in getting a scrap of an idea into a living, breathing thing – be it a business, book, service or campaign.

Celebration notwithstanding, I also love the opportunity to run around with a checklist and a clipboard, and the planning that goes along with event management makes my type-A, control-freak, detail-fixated self happy as the proverbial Larry.

Event basics checklist:

- Why are you asking people to leave their nests to attend your event? What do you want to achieve from holding an event? Is it increased sales? Increased brand exposure? Media coverage?

- What is the format and tone of this event? Casual, formal, structured, informative, entertaining? What catering will complement this?

- When are you having it? Can your clients/guests actually get to your event on the date and time you would like it? Are there any other competing events at that time/date?

- Where are you celebrating? Does your proposed venue have adequate parking and access? Is there enough space for your guest list? Can your caterers do their job easily and effectively? Is there space for your media and speaking guests? Do you need to hire seating?

- Who's on your invitation and speaking list? Current and future clients, colleagues, influencers, friends and family?

- How will the event unfold? Yep, I'm talking a running sheet. Even the most unstructured event with no formalities, speeches or otherwise still needs a running sheet to ensure all the logistics are managed, giving your guests/attendees an enjoyable experience that looks seamless from their perspective. Another 'how' involves budget – how much cashola do you have to allocate to this event?

The answers to those questions will inform a promotional plan.

The level of promotion and marketing you apply to your event depends entirely on the structure and purpose of your event. It may be as simple as designing or buying a set of beautiful invitations for you to either mail out electronically or through old school post. An event that's aligned to a sales goal will need more strategic promotion and marketing, which may involve Facebook ads, media relations campaigns and a dedicated mailing list email campaign, plotted out against milestones with calendar-based deadlines for distribution.

Here's a bonus step: if it's your launch celebration – outsource its management! It's hard to swan around with a glass of bubbles when you have the caterer asking you for cling wrap, or your guest speaker busting your chops for a car park. Bask in your glory, because you have created something fabulous that deserves an equally fabulous launch!

Partner up and collaborate

There are so many benefits to collaborating. I've seen some wonderful, mutually beneficial results that can be achieved through people in business partnering up, playing nice and delivering beautiful projects. Working in business can sometimes feel professionally isolating, so an effective collaboration can provide that sense of teamwork that comes from equitably splitting up a project's workload and expenses and having a shared commitment to the outcome. The right collaboration will feel inspirational and motivating. There's a sense of connection with your collaborator as you work towards your shared desired outcome, and the process of working with someone else exposes you to new techniques and approaches and a fresh perspective.

A collaboration is a means to grow your network. You'll meet new people (prospective clients) with someone in your corner who's helping you build awareness of your brand. A successful collaboration has the potential to significantly grow your business by giving you access to double your usual audience for a project.

People power

Of course, a collaboration doesn't have to be limited to person to person, business to business. Business/person to community organisation is also a wonderful way to connect via a sponsorship, one which will increase brand awareness and loyalty while giving a lovely dose of the feels.

I'm a fan of ye olde sponsorship of a community event – it's an opportunity to work with the local community to support them in achieving their goals, all while raising the profile of your business in a positive light.

Feels aside, sponsorship is a business deal, not just a donation, and needs to be strategically aligned with both your business goals and your communications strategy. It's important, nay essential to determine the right sponsorship partnership for your business:

- Does the prospective sponsorship recipient have a marketing plan in place to promote your involvement and support? What opportunities are there for cross-promotion?

- Does the prospective sponsorship recipient have demographics that are aligned to your ideal client?

- What is the competitive environment like?
  Specifically, do they have other businesses like
  yours supporting their organisation?

- How will they use your sponsorship?

Sponsorship is a communications tactic that I often
prescribe to clients, providing, of course, that the
organisation they're supporting is aligned to their
business values and positioning. If I had a client
that specialised in burlesque (to put it delicately), I
wouldn't be encouraging them to donate a tassel-
twirling package to the local school fair silent
auction. However, if a client's target audience is
families, then yes, absolutely, donate a term of
dance classes to the child care centre annual raffle.

If you are considering a donation, before you
become entranced by the super-cute, gap-toothed
kid saying with a lisp, 'We need pink paint or there'll
be no unicorns and our dreams will be crushed,' it's
a good idea to set a number of ground rules for your
donation, as well as some ground rules for yourself:

- Set a deadline for services (e.g. within six
  months) and be willing to extend at least once.

- Find out who won the item after the event.
  Contact them to thank them and schedule an
  initial meeting or consultation to encourage
  their take up of the donation.

- Be absolutely clear on what is being provided. For example – hours, number of appointments.

- Think about donating several smaller prizes rather than one big one, to the same value of what you are comfortable donating. This could result in gaining more long-term clients.

- Depending on your donation type, if appropriate, position the donation as an introductory consultation to determine whether or not you want to begin an ongoing business relationship with the winner.

- Promote your involvement via your own social networks.

- Use compelling copy to describe your donation.

Go forth and kill two birds with the one communications stone – support your local community and meet some strategic objectives such as brand awareness and loyalty. Plus, the feels. Never discount the feels. Ah, altruism – there's no warm and fuzzy like it. Except maybe a poochy. They're pretty warm and fuzzy. I should know – there's one constantly sitting on my feet.

Old school communications

Stop Press!

I'm often asked about the effectiveness of a media release as a communications tool, and my answer varies depending on the campaign or business in question. I'd rarely advise against an effective media relations campaign that supports an overarching marketing and communications plan. A good campaign will drive up customer numbers and strengthen and increase a brand profile in the local community and further afield. However, bitter experience means I would advise against pinning all communications and business hopes and dreams on a single release. The best release in the world cannot compete with the public disclosure of a footballer sleeping with a co-player's wife. *she says, lower lip slightly trembling, the pain as acute now as it was almost two decades ago*

A well-written media release that's *irresistable* to journos is such a fantastic communications tool to build your brand awareness and enhance your credibility as an expert in your field. Free publicity, people!

Key elements of a killer media release

Newsworthiness

Why would a journalist be interested in promoting your business? Journos aren't usually in the business of advertising, so in order to pique their interest, your story needs to:

- Elicit an emotional response
- Address a current social or economic issue; or
- Be of benefit or harm to others

Enticing headline

It needs to be short and sharp, and convey the content within the body of the release itself. Here's where I deviate from many copywriters – I can't write a headline until I've written the copy. For me, the headline will be unearthed from the process of writing the release.

Brevity

Keep your release to one page if possible, not including your bio. If you have a ton of information to support the claims in your release, or it's part of a bigger project, write a fact or briefing sheet that gives an overview of the background and status of your project.

Structure

We've all seen the editor in a million movies shouting, 'Just gimme the facts, ma'am,' and the introductory paragraphs of your media release should include the relevant Who, What, Where, How and Why information. Lead strong, my warrior, and structure your release so the main juicy content is at the start of your release, so the journalist reading it thinks, 'Oh my goodness, I HAVE to give this story my full and absolute consideration!' Do this, then back up your introductory statement and claims with detail throughout the rest of the body of your release. Finish with your contact details.

Images

If you have access to images to support your story (and good images, professionally shot), mention that in your pitch. A publication may be willing to send a journalist to meet with you, but if they don't need a photographer, that can sway in your favour.

Flyers, letterboxes and cafes, oh my!

I bet that right now, if you call into your local cafe to pick up a double-shot latte, you'll leave with a shot of business writing muse on the side. While waiting for your order, jittery and edgy, cast your eyes over the spread of flyers, brochures and business cards promoting local businesses. Inspiration granted – is there nothing a barista cannot do?

A promotional flyer can be a fantastic tool in your strategic communications toolkit – as long as it's part of a broader strategy, of course, and not a random letterbox drop. Ugh … More on that shortly, but for now, many businesses feel as though they should have a flyer of some description, but for what purpose? Is it to introduce your business, to raise awareness, to promote a specific service you have developed or an event you are having?

The flyer has to be good. It's a representation of your business, so for the love of God and all that is holy in the world of communications, have your flyer professionally designed. Now isn't the time for you to have a crack at playing around with fonts. A graphic designer will ensure your flyer looks good and is branded correctly. This extends to the actual words on your flyer. Cut out all the unnecessary fluff, get your key messages front and centre, and ensure your flyer contains all the information it needs to for maximum impact. Write to your audience and make sure your grammar and spelling are impeccable. Proof the plucking daylights out of the copy – including contact details!

Further to this, your flyer needs a strong call to action message. This could be directing readers to your website for further information, a request for social media engagement, or a 'phone to make an appointment' directive. Many businesses offer an incentive to elicit responses – we've all seen the 'mention this ad for 20% off' messages on marketing materials. If you choose this path, add conditions to your incentive or make sure it's an incentive you are comfortable to implement.

All that done? Big box of flyers blocking your doorway? Now what? I know that although keen for a flyer in their communications toolkit, people often have limited plans on how to get them into the hands of clients and customers, other than pulling on the sneakers and letterbox dropping them all over the local neighbourhood. So, I hereby present to you, dear reader, my thoughts on letterbox drops.

Short answer – I'm not a fan. I don't like eco-unfriendly marketing full stop, but beyond this, letterbox drops are an expensive form of marketing that has the potential to be scattergun. My elderly neighbour is regularly invited to kindergarten open days, even though she represents a household with zero interest, desire or need for early childhood services. Once a month, I have a flyer in my

mailbox offering me a discount to have my roof retiled –
which would be relevant if I didn't have a Colorbond metal
roof. It's much more effective to identify where your target
audience is hanging out and hit them directly there.

That's my naysayer response. Now for some positivity. You
have a beautiful flyer promoting your business that appeals
to a wide audience, you want to work with a localised
community and you're desperate to get out in the fresh
air. There's a massive feel-good factor in supporting local
businesses, which can be capitalised on through a letterbox
campaign. Pop on your Fitbit, and off you go!

CHAPTER SIXTEEN

Every Communication Counts

Win them back with beautiful business writing

Every contact a business or organisation has with an audience is an opportunity to knock off socks with good communications, Dr Seuss vibe optional, of course.

I have a number of clients with member-based businesses (think gyms, educational services, peak bodies), and renewal and retention is an ongoing process which can be delicate at the best of times. If a business is poised to significantly increase pricing, then the delicacy level is right up there. Price rises are unavoidable, and clients are often understandably concerned about the potential backlash. Good communications and beautiful writing cushions the renewal process, but it's also an opportunity to reconnect, and to show some love.

My advice is always, ALWAYS avoid just sending an invoice with the updated amount and hope for the best. Rather, craft a piece of content that answers the most basic of questions: 'What's in it for me?' This involves reaching out to the readers' motivation and making the membership so enticing that price increase is irrelevant.

A thoughtfully crafted piece of membership content has five sections:

1. Open with a thank you and recognition.

2. Clear articulation of the value and benefits of being part of the business.

3. Upcoming plans with a ton of enthusiasm and excitement for upcoming projects, plans and events.

4. A clear call to action with a stupidly easy process to take next steps.

5. Finally, a repeated statement of gratitude with a point of contact for any queries or further information, stressing that the business is looking forward to another great year.

Five little paragraphs can avoid a whole lot of potential pain and show a ton of love.

Another potential target for an approach like this is lapsed and former members and clients. They are often an untapped potential audience. Almost all organisations and businesses have some form of KPIs focusing on recruitment and retention in their annual business plans, be it more members, more clients, more sales. Thus, it makes sense to check in on a regular basis with those who have shown an interest in the organisation previously, in whatever context, be it previous members, people who have made a product enquiry or former clients or customers.

Something initially attracted them to the business/ organisation, perhaps a recognition that 'these are my people.' For whatever reason, they left, but if the perceived benefit and initial attraction element are clearly and appropriately articulated, then they may be enticed back into the fold.

The campaign would need minimal tweaking in terms of copy – maybe just a rework that highlights changes to the business, future directions and a direct, welcoming invitation for involvement. This basic concept can be applied across all business types, and it's a proven approach used by some of the biggest businesses in the country. Not a week goes by without Blue51 HQ receiving a 'we miss you' letter from a telco or an energy company. Awww, bless them and their door-knocking working-holiday backpackers …

Track and measure; track and measure!

Track and measure; measure and track. It's something I bang on about All. The. Time. Seriously, I bore myself, but tracking and measurement are so essential to my communications that I feel more than slightly jittery when clients tell me that they've never looked at their Google Analytics *shudders involuntarily then vomits into a handbag, not necessarily her own*.

I get it; the measuring is so much less fun than the doing and the getting it done. Sometimes it involves spreadsheets *she vomits again*. By the time the measurement stage in a project comes around, we're already over it and onto the next thing. Tactic measurement and evaluation was a huge focus in one of my early communications roles, when I used to totter around in skyscraper heels and my knees didn't make a peep. My communications director at the time used to say (i.e. basically yell) in every campaign planning meeting, 'If you can't measure it, it doesn't exist.'

It's true; if you're not tracking a response, then how do you know if something is worth repeating, if it's working against your objective? How do you know if what you're putting out in the world is hitting its mark?

You've done the Word Nerd part; now it's time for your inner Numbers Nerd to shine. Release the numbers! Track and measure, my pretty, and make the process easy by jumping into your Google Analytics dashboard. Google Analytics is a must for your communications toolkit. It's a free tool that monitors your website performance in terms of traffic, keywords and audience. It has so much info and data that cannot only be used to improve your website, but also guide your broader communications strategy.

That said, Google Analytics can be extremely overwhelming and potentially confusing, particularly for a Word Nerd like me who has a reverse-Pavlovian response to charts and spreadsheets. In my first year of having it installed, I think I glanced at it sporadically, put it in the f*ckit bucket and slunk away quietly, avoiding eye contact. But like any good

Word Nerd using content marketing as a cornerstone of my communications strategy, I had to get comfortable with data (spreadsheets and charts, bleugh) and know that the effort I was putting into my content was actually yielding results. Enter some quick training to be able to navigate my way around the dashboard, and off I went.

First things first – your Analytics will yield a lot of data. A LOT. There are a few key metrics relevant to the majority of businesses that I work with, including my own:

Traffic source

Where are people coming to your website from? Your social media platforms? Organic search? Directly? The answers to this should guide any tweaks and changes to your social media strategy. For example, if Facebook has a low referral source percentage, try adding more direct shares from specific pages in your website, or play around with your calls to action on posts.

Audience

Where is your audience based? If you're strictly a location-based business, then your keywords should reflect that (e.g. Business writing workshops Melbourne). What are their demographics? Are they reflecting those of your ideal client? How many visitors are returning? A high(ish) return rate may indicate people are connecting with your content. #yay

Search terms

What terms are leading people to your website? Are they the terms that you expect? I use this metric to confirm and guide my keywords when I'm tweaking my content strategy. They can prompt new ideas of content I hadn't considered, as well as ensure that I'm writing to a purpose rather than just taking a stab in the dark.

Behaviour

What pages have the highest visits? Where are people lingering, and where are they bouncing? Does this reflect your goals for your website?

I'm creative. I love writing, and numbers give me the heebie-jeebies. Weirdly, though, I love tracking. It confirms (and sometimes refutes) my speculated understandings about audiences and their behaviour. I use it to measure the impact of social media or email campaigns, to keep on top of search behaviour and to align my (or my client's) target audience information against online communications.

One of the things I most love about online communications is its fluidity. It's not like spending $12k for a billboard campaign and crossing your fingers that your ideal client will just happen to drive along that highway at the right time. Every piece of content can be manipulated, tweaked, edited, added to and improved upon. Look at your results and then adjust your activities. Easy!

PART FIVE

Like a Boss

CHAPTER SEVENTEEN

Pulling it all Together

OK, let's recap your movement through this book in your quest for storytelling glory. You've thought about your ideal audience, you've brainstormed a list of stories to share with them so they can connect with your message, and in Part Three: Stories in Action, you've thought about some tactics what will hit that audience right where it hurts. Now it's time to plot out the when.

Keep in mind that some of your tactics will be ongoing; some will be once-off. Your mailing list opt-ins, for example, you might decide to repeat every quarter, or you might like to create and release a different one each month. Again, at the risk of repeating myself (again), every tactic needs to be aligned to your goals. If building your mailing list isn't essential to your business growth, then don't worry about adding a strategy against it.

Ready for your plan of attack? Let's build this mofo!

Turning goals into actions

- Get thyself a big wall planner.

- Go back to chapter one where I asked you to outline your business and communications goals. Allocate your goals for the year equally across quarters against relevant milestones. This becomes your action plan!

- Break the associated tactics, activities and tasks into actions via a project planning tool like KANBAN or Asana.

- Get down and dirty with the details – seriously plot out each step so you can see what's involved. Add deadlines and due dates for each step that are plotted into your calendar. Don't overload or overwhelm yourself – space them out so you can achieve your goals without cancelling Christmas.

- Review, review, review!

Day-to-day of being your own communications director

So, are we done? Yes and no. Unfortunately, a communications plan isn't a set-and-forget piece of work. It requires a bit of love and attention to get the very most out of your efforts and turn your gorgeous action plan into, well, action!

I've been doing this long enough now to have some tried and tested tricks up my sleeve for getting sh*t done when motivation is lacking:

1. Set goals, then go forth and smash them

Each month, have yourself a communications meeting to review your stats and communications key metrics, such as email open rates, social media stats and leads or enquiries. Revisit your quarterly goals, looking ahead to the next quarter. Most importantly, reward yourself! Maybe not a three-hour liquid lunch, but something lovely at your favourite cafe.

2. Embrace the to-do list

Each week, I have a planning meeting where I set my communications goals for the week and write down (in ye olde school notebook) everything that needs to be completed for the week ahead, which is then entered into my daily schedule. I love that smug, self-satisfied feeling of ticking off an item.

3. Re-energise thyself frequently

I like to work in blocks of time (Pomodoro-esque as a nod to my Italian heritage), and after each block, I take a break. I get away from my desk and put on a load of washing, I call a friend and chat about anything non-work-related, or I sit out in the sun with a coffee or water and my dog and just chill. I also like to work from a cafe or a client's office from time to time, just to mix it up a bit.

4. Maintain a beautiful workspace

I'm naturally neat and organised, and clutter does my head in. Having a beautiful, well-organised workspace means my office is a space I want to be in.

5. Create external deadlines

If I've promised a delivery date, then I'll bust my hump to deliver, motivation or no. It's that simple. Apply the same concept to your own communications.

CHAPTER EIGHTEEN

A Note on Bravery

Telling your story isn't easy, especially in the context of promoting yourself. It can feel decidedly icky and it takes real courage to put yourself out there, particularly when your Instagram feed is full of thinly veiled humble brags, faux vulnerability and 'authenticity'.

It can be intimidating, using your story to connect with your ideal client, especially if you feel like your grasp of grammar isn't the best, or if you were steered away from seeing yourself as a strong writer either at school or in the early stages of your career. Many people I work with shy away from telling their story because of fear of judgement, of being misunderstood, and sometimes fear of not being able to do justice via their writing skills to the value they bring.

Here's the thing – true vulnerability is as uncomfortable to experience as it is compelling to witness, and as I have explained through these pages, nothing connects like a story. So please, tell yours.

And they lived happily ever after

I'd love to hear about your business writing projects, so please don't hesitate to reach out to me and let me know how you are going. In the meantime, you'll find a truckload of small business communications and writing resources on my website. I regularly share my insights, events and communications tips and tricks with my mailing list, and I'd love you to jump aboard, also via my website. Boo yeah!

If you'd like more practical support with your business communications and writing, I offer a range of services, as hands on (or not) as you require. Please email me at hello@ blue51.com.au for more information.

186 | *Holly Cardamone*

About the Author

Holly Cardamone is a Melbourne-based writer, communications specialist and all-round Word Nerd who works with people to tell their story and grow their brand using beautiful communications. Through her consultancy, Blue51 Communications, Holly provides strategic and specialist communications support and writing services. She writes anything and everything, almost always with a smile on her face, a coffee within grasp and a space-invading Australian Shepherd on her feet.

Holly earned her postgraduate Master of Arts (Communications) at Swinburne University, chased up by her Master of Arts (Professional Writing and Literature) at Deakin University.

A committed long-term niche-dodger, she has worked with businesses and organisations of all sizes and sectors to clarify their message and connect with their ideal clients to get the results they desire and deserve. She's down to earth, smart as a whip and funny to boot with the ability to cut to the core of a story with practical, relevant and solutions-focused specialist advice and support.

Holly is a wife to a devilishly handsome Carlton Football Club tragic, mama to two feisty cherubs and her favourite place is waterside. She's a lifelong language connoisseur, a mostly inconspicuous eavesdropper, a voracious reader, a potty mouth, an almost fearless box jumper (Google it) and is hands down the person you want on your table at a trivia night.

Contact

LinkedIn:
www.linkedin.com/in/hollycardamone/

Instagram:
www.instagram.com/blue51_holly/

Facebook:
www.facebook.com/
Blue51CommunicationsConsultancy/

Website:
www.blue51.com.au/

Email:
hello@blue51.com.au

www.ingramcontent.com/pod-product-compliance
Lightning Source LLC
Chambersburg PA
CBHW071549200326
41519CB00021BB/6664